SECRETS OF THE HERRIN GANGS

An Inside Account of Bloody Williamson

By RALPH JOHNSON

*Former employee of both **Charlie Birger** and the **Shelton Gang**
in the Roaring Twenties as told to Paul H. Hayward in 1927*

And JON MUSGRAVE

*With new research on the criminal exploits of the man behind
the Ralph Johnson pseudonym — Max B. Pulliam*

Published by
IllinoisHistory.com
PO Box 1142
Marion IL 62959

Front Cover
Newspaper clippings of the Rome Club (bottom) where a meeting of the Knights of the Flaming Circle took place on Feb. 8, 1924, leading to a series of events that night that included the murder of Caesar Cagle on East Cherry Street (top) in front of the Jefferson Hotel in Herrin, Ill. Mug shots (l-r) show Monroe "Blackie" Armes, Max "Pat" Pulliam and Bernie Shelton. Finger print record from Pulliam's inmate file at Leavenworth Penitentiary.

Back Cover
Mug shots (l-r) show Carl Shelton, Monroe "Blackie" Armes, Marshall McCormack and Charles "Blackie" Harris. Paperwork from Pulliam's inmate file at Leavenworth.

Newspaper clippings courtesy of the *Herrin City Library | Local History Room*. Mug shots and paperwork from the Leavenworth Penitentiary Records at the *National Archives — Kansas City*.

Cover Design
Jon Musgrave

Library of Congress Control Number: 2010937522

International Standard Book Number (ISBN)
paperback: 978-0-9707984-9-7

Printed in the United States of America
2nd printing

Foreword

It's hard to believe some of the stories that came out of "Bloody Williamson" and for good reason. Many simply aren't true. Most are exaggerated and the details are often wrong. Truth in advertising, the same could be said for the contents of this book, but we're talking about a five-year span of one of the bloodiest decades in American history when it comes to organized mobs and criminal gangs. More than 70 people lost their lives in and around Williamson from the Herrin Massacre in 1922 up through Charlie Birger's hanging in 1928.

Much of the violence took place with the gangs of Charlie Birger and Shelton Brothers on one side, or by the end, on opposite sides.

"Ralph Johnson" whoever he was, had an inside view of the Shelton Gang for quite a while and this is his story first published in January 1927. First he sold his story to the *St. Louis Star*, then to the NEA wire service which divided it into a 10-part series that ran in newspapers across the country later that month.

For the first time, Johnson's 9,000-word account has been combined in one volume transcribed from four different newspapers, the *Sheboygan Press* of Wisconsin, the *Newark Advocate* of Newark, Ohio, the *Lima News* of Lima, Ohio, and the *Ironwood Daily Globe* of Ironwood, Mich.

Johnson wasn't the only gangster looking to get out and cash out. Art Newman and Connie Ritter followed in the *St. Louis Post-Dispatch* later that same month. The difference appears to be in the accuracy. Neither of the latter two men had been with Charlie Birger long. Newman for just over three months and Ritter maybe another four or five. They didn't know much about Birger's early career. They had also just taken part in a number of murders with Birger and used the story to shift blame to other parties and set up their alibis.

Johnson didn't seem to have that problem. He simply didn't have the blood on his hands as those two. The press didn't consider him a major player and he could likely have gone unnoticed by the law had he reversed his ways. While he notes up front that Johnson isn't his real name I believe he was likely Max "Pat" Pulliam, a Shelton gangster from Franklin County, who would have been 28 years old at the time. New research shows he had worked as a reporter possibly before and definitely after his time with the gang. Later news accounts identified him as the owner of the slot machines involved in the gang disputes. Johnson didn't say he owned them, but did admit he worked as the collector for the Sheltons and Birger when the two gangs were still aligned. That and the reference at one point to his young wife adds to the theory.

The publication of the series came at a thrilling time for newspaper readers. The stories ran just after the burning of Birger's notorious resort, Shady Rest, but before the Sheltons went on trial in federal court at the end of the month for a mail robbery two years earlier. During this time "Bloody Williamson" still generated headlines with the kidnapping and disappearance of state highway patrolman Lory Price and his wife Ethel, as well as the assumed suicide a few days later of "Gang Queen" Helen Holbrook, who had affairs with both Birger and Carl Shelton. She too had been planning to sell her inside story at the time of her death.

As I mentioned at the beginning of this foreword, let me

forewarn, not everything Johnson wrote is true. Many of the earlier accounts have the feel of hearsay and that he's reporting second hand. Likewise, he has a number of small errors, especially dates, that are probably off due to relying on the faulty memory of himself or his original sources in the gang.

Still, his account is one of the original sources historians have used for decades. It reveals behind the scenes clues that never made it into the contemporary news stories. As a researcher it's rare to find such an inside account, especially one as readable as Johnson's. Both leading biographies of Charlie Birger and the Shelton Brothers, Gary DeNeal's, *A Knight of Another Sort*, and Taylor Pensoneau's, *Brothers Notorious*, use Johnson's account most likely from copies of the *St. Louis Star* articles in the Paul Angle papers at the Chicago Historical Society. Angle's papers and notes compiled for his *Bloody Williamson* represent a treasure trove for researchers of the period. Yet, ironically, Angle's work which just skimmed the surface of what actually happened in Southern Illinois, never mentioned Johnson by name.

Although his story never made it into book form in 1927, others did, especially as the year progressed. Multiple trials and confessions revealed ever more detailed accounts of what had actually happened. Williamson County Sheriff George Galligan survived both the Klan War and the Gang War. When his four-year term ended in December 1926, he wrote *In Bloody Williamson* with the help of his special deputy Jack Wilkinson. Focusing on his role fighting the Ku Klux Klan, he and Wilkinson used the book's proceeds to help the widow of his late Chief Deputy Ora Thomas who had been killed in a shootout with the leading Klan raider.

As the trials progress two more booklets came out. E. Bishop

Hill wrote *The Complete History of the Southern Illinois Gang War*, which really wasn't that complete, and the Illinois Book Co., under the leadership of *Marion Daily Republican* Publisher Oldham Paisley put out anonymously, *The Life Story of Charlie Birger: History of the Crimes of the Birger Gang*. Either Paisley or young reporter Homer Butler (or more likely both) probably wrote the book. With Birger and many of his henchmen on trial for the murder of Joe Adams and later Ward "Casey" Jones and Lyle "Shag" Worsham, editorial focus turned to Birger and his gang, allowing the Sheltons to slip away to a great extent. Those trials took place locally in Marion and Benton. The Shelton trials took place in Quincy in western Illinois, and at Taylorville in the central part of the state.

The Shelton's big trials after the Gang War, the Collinsville mail robbery and Kinkaid bank robbery relied heavily on the most likely perjured testimony of Art Newman. Their trials revealed little of the inner workings of their side of the story.

The Williamson County Historical Society in Marion, Illinois has reprints of the last three books available for sale. It's in the same spirit of offering this voice from the past that Johnson's story is being retold.

As such, I think you'll find it is worth reading and I hope you enjoy.

Jon Musgrave
IllinoisHistory.com
September 20 , 2010

By Ralph Johnson

Former Member of the Shelton Gang as Told to Paul H. Hayward

Chapter 1

This is the story of the gangs of "Bloody Williamson" county — the gangs and their fights, their rum-running business and the war they have been waging for two years.

There are two gangs in Williamson county, Illinois — the Shelton gang and the Birger gang. Between them, they have made a whole lot of money, taken a lot of lives and flooded southern Illinois with a lot of liquor — besides giving the city of Herrin a black eye all over the country.

The Shelton gang was the first on the scene. Three brothers — Carl, Earl and Bernie — started it. They came from Wayne county, Ill., and have two other brothers who never mixed in with their gang deals.

In 1923 Earl Shelton, who had been a coal miner, started a booze joint, which was a road house and gambling den combined at a crossroads between Carterville and Fordville, Ill.[1] The criminal history of the Shelton gang dates from the day that road house opened.

Carl and Bernie joined hands with him. It wasn't long before they had built up a whisky-hauling organization that made them the kingpins of all the middle western rum runners. Then came

---

[1] Other references place the joint at the Carterville-Colp crossroads. Fordville was an early name for the village of Energy, Ill. The post office had changed to Energy in 1913.

the beginning of the warfare that has startled the country. First the Sheltons fought the kluxers. Then Charlie Birger organized his gang, and the two gangs shot it out every time they met.

Now Earl and Bernie are in jail accused of the Collinsville mail robbery, and Carl is out under bond on the same charge, hiding in East St. Louis to keep away from Birger.

To begin with, my real name isn't Ralph Johnson, although I went under the name of Johnson during most of the time that I was a member of the Shelton gang. Naturally I don't want my real name used now. I'm out of the racket for good now, I hope, and I'm looking for an honest job. The racket isn't what it used to be. The coal mines are all working, but the people just aren't spending their money like they did.

Then this war between the Sheltons and Birger has shot things up. And with the Shelton brothers either in jail or hiding out, I had to clear out or get knocked off. Besides, I got married a year or so ago, and ever since the little woman's been after me to quit the racket. So I have.

We'll start this story with the opening of the Sheltons' road house in 1923. Business was good that fall. The Williamson county mines were all working and money was plentiful. The dice table and booze business at the Shelton place were showing good profits and everything was jake. Bernie Shelton, youngest of the brothers was operating a taxi cab in Carterville.

Then, early in January, 1924, the Ku Klux Klan got in business in Williamson county, and the peaceful days were over. Glenn Young, a former U.S. revenue officer, was brought into the region by the Kluxers to help their "clean-up" campaign. [2]

---

[2] Actually, the Klan publicly revealed themselves in Williamson County during the last week of May 1923.

They started off easy, raiding a few small roadhouses. Then, toward the last of January, came a raid on the Shelton place.[3]

Young, Harry Walker and Caesar Cagle led the klux raiders, who came in with drawn pistols. They lined the Sheltons and the guests up against the wall, ransacked the place and confiscated the roll of bills from the crap game.

"I've a good notion to kill you," growled Walker, waving his gun under Earl Shelton's nose. "You know I can do it too."

"You've got the best of me now," says Earl, his hands high in the air. "But don't think this is the end of it. I won't forget."

Then the raiders drove everybody out and set fire to the place. The roadhouse and two autos parked outside were burned.

Earl Shelton was as good as his word. He didn't forget, and that raid wasn't the end of it. It was only the beginning.

Bernie and Carl Shelton gave up their other jobs to rally 'round with Earl. With them came Jack Skelcher and Charley Briggs, a couple of men who had used guns ever since they were kids.

About a week after the raid, Williamson county saw the organization of the Knights of the Flaming Circle to flight the Klan.[4] Enthusiasm ran high, at first, although later one, when things got pretty hot, nearly everybody in the Flaming Circle would remember some other pressing engagement when a call went out to gather for a scrap.

But anyhow, it was a live outfit then. And it wasn't long before things began to happen.

---

[3] The Klan first held its first raid Dec. 22, 1923, then more on Jan. 5, 7, 20, and Feb. 1, 1924. Newspapers don't show which raid targeted Shelton, but on Jan. 9, Shelton swore out warrants against Young, Walker, Cagle, Carl Neilson and a fifth man named Carlson, charging the five with larceny. This would suggest Young's raid against Shelton probably took place on the 5th or the 7th.

[4] The Flaming Circle had actually held its first public auto procession on Sept. 10, 1923.

The lounger turned suddenly,
whipped out a pistol and fired
point blank at the Klux raider

Chapter 2

It wasn't long after the raid on the Shelton brothers roadhouse before things began to happen.

Caesar Cagle, one of the leaders in the raid was strolling down the main street in Herrin the night of Feb. 8, 1924. A man lounged past him as he came abreast of the Jefferson hotel.

Without warning the lounger turned suddenly, whipped out a pistol and fired point-blank at the Klux raiders. At the same time another man coming up from behind drew a gun and shot Cagle in the back. "This was the favorite method of disposing of an enemy in Herrin."

Cagle went down dead. The gunmen lit out. Bystanders picked up Cagle. He had two pistols in his belt and he wore a sweater that was identified as having belonged to Jack Skelcher, the Sheltons right bower before the raid.[5]

That was the beginning of the gang war shootings.

A Flight to Florida

Right after it the three Sheltons with Skelcher and Charley Briggs, a hard-boiled, two-gun man, left Illinois in a hurry, by auto, landing in Jacksonville, Fla. They hung around Jacksonville for several months before they drifted back to East St. Louis and as soon as they got back to Illinois trouble started again.

S. Glenn Young, leader of the kluxers and then chief raider, started from Herrin with Mrs. Young on an auto trip to St. Louis a few days after the Sheltons had returned. As his car reached the

---

[5] According to Webster a "right bower" is "the knave of the trump suit, the highest card (except the "Joker") in the game." In other words, Skelcher served as one of their top lieutenants.

Washington-Clinton county line in the Okaw river bottoms, another car swept up from behind.

Five men in the other car opened fire, with automatics and shotguns. Mrs. Young got a charge of buckshot in the face. Young was wounded several times but managed to bring his car to a halt, just at the crest of a twenty-foot embankment, before he collapsed. The other car went on and disappeared.

Passersby took the Young to a hospital where both recovered. On the next day Skelcher and Briggs set out to drive from East St. Louis to Herrin. Just as they entered Williamson county a band of armed men, afterwards identified as kluxers told them to halt. Briggs, who was at the wheel, stepped on the gas, and they sped away in a shower of lead.

A few hundred yards away down the road, however, another car coming from the opposite direction stopped them.[6] Skelcher threw up his hands as the pursuers came up. It didn't help him any, though — he was instantly killed by a rifle ball through the body. Briggs jumped out and started to run but was shot through the hip and captured.

Taken to a Herrin hospital, he was jailed three days later charged with a part in the shooting of Young. At the same time Earl and Carl Shelton were pinched in East St. Louis on the same charge. Apparently Young had failed to note the presence of Bernie Shelton, the third brother among his assailants.

Young Goes Barnstorming

Briggs and the Sheltons were soon released on bail. This made

---

[6] The story passed down in Skelcher's family places the incident on the Herrin-Colp highway where it crossed the Illinois Central R.R. Today, this is just east of the intersection of Taylor St. (the old highway alignment) and 26th St. [Sept. 6, 2010. Phone interview with Jack Morris.]

Young furious. He telephoned Sheriff Ragan at Carlyle, Ill., where the Sheltons had been in jail.

"I told you to keep them Sheltons in jail," Young yelled. "I'm through with you double-crossers, and I won't have anything more to do with you."

Thereupon Young, heavily guarded set off on an auto junket through northern Illinois, Wisconsin and Minnesota, exhibiting his bullet-riddled auto to throngs along the way for ten cents a look. So we were rid of him for a while.

But the calm didn't last. The two Sheltons were arrested for the killing of Caesar Cagle.

They were soon discharged because of lack in evidence, and immediately afterwards Sheriff George Galligan had his deputy Bud Allison go to the Herrin garage of John Smith, an ardent kluxer, to reclaim the auto of Jack Skelcher and turn it over to Jack's brother, Buck.[7]

The Bloodiest Battle of All

Bud asked the Shelton boys to go with him.[8] They got a dozen or more of the friends, all heavily armed and the whole bunch tromped down the street to Smith's garage.

They walked straight into what turned out to be the bloodiest battle of the whole Williamson county war.

---

[7] The car didn't belong to Skelcher's brother. It had actually been stolen from a businessman at Cobden, Ill., who wanted it returned. Brother "Buck" was one of Jack's older brothers, Dwight L. Skelcher, who had been arrested in 1922 for robbing the bank in Thompsonville, Ill. [Oct. 5, 1922. "Two Suspected Bank Robbers Under Arrest." *Benton Republican* (Benton, Ill.). 1.]

[8] Bud was the nickname for James Robert Allison, born on March 26, 1876, in Alabama. Newspaper accounts almost always got the name wrong, using either A. J., or J. H. His death certificate in Williamson County lists J. R. Allison. [World War I Draft Registration Cards, 1917-1918, Ancestry.com; 1900, 1910 and 1920 Censuses of Jefferson Co., Alabama; and Illinois Statewide Death Index, 1916-1950. Illinois State Archives. Secretary of State website.

Chapter 3

There were nearly a dozen armed men in the group that walked down Monroe St., in Herrin, behind the Shelton brothers that afternoon, bound for John Smith's garage to get Jack Skelcher's auto. Deputy Sheriff Bud Allison led the way.[9]

Smith was an ardent klansman, and his garage was a sort of center for klan activities. That was why we all went armed. It was a good thing we did.

There was a grape arbor in a yard across the street from the garage. As the crowd walked up to the garage three shots rang out from this arbor. Bud Allison fell dead, shot through the head and the body. And the Shelton gang went into action, pronto.

Everybody had his gun out. From a dozen vantage points in the vicinity of the garage hidden klansmen fired back.

A squadron of autos filled with klansmen came down the street. Earl Shelton, his face black with anger, ran to the street intersection, squatted behind a concrete traffic post and, with drawn revolvers, forced the drivers to detour to right and left. The klan outfit at the garage thus failed to get its expected reinforcements.

Movie Stuff

Carl Shelton, dripping blood from a bullet wound in the left

---

[9] Johnson's account of the first shootout at Smith's Garage on Aug. 30, 1924, differs greatly from Sheriff George Galligan's own account from his "In Bloody Williamson" book. However, the sheriff's account also differs greatly from the Klan-backed testimony at the coroner's inquest. The actual truth of what took place that day will likely never be completely revealed. By the use of the pronoun "we" Johnson implies that he took part in this incident. Johnson completely leaves out the presence of Galligan and another deputy Ora Thomas who were also present.

arm, went down an alley and entered the grape arbor from behind. He found Green Dunning, an Oklahoma two-gun man imported by the klan, kneeling there with a smoking pistol in each hand. Darting up behind him, Carl threw one arm around his neck and jammed his revolver into his back.

"Give up, you ____ ___ _ ____," yelled Carl.

"Not until I'm dead, damn you," retorted Dunning.

At that minute a man named Blackburn, one of the Shelton gang, came up. He put the muzzle of his gun against Dunning's head, and again Carl asked Dunning if he would give up. Again Dunning shouted defiance.

Blackburn pulled the trigger and that was the end of Dunning.[10]

Six Casualties

Suddenly the fusillade of shots died away. Deputy sheriffs had a Browning machine gun hidden in the Palace hotel, and had brought it out and made themselves masters of the situation. The rival gunmen drew away to count their losses and bind up their wounds.

Six men lost their lives — Dunning, Allison, Charley Wollard, Bert Wollard (an innocent bystander), and a klansman and a Shelton gang member whose names I can't remember. Herman Phemister, another of the Shelton gang, died a couple of weeks later of his wounds.[11]

---

[10] Johnson never goes on to describe Mr. Blackburn further which may suggest that he was still alive and free. There were a number of Blackburn males in Williamson County living at that time who could have been associated with the Sheltons.

[11] Other accounts don't mention a Bert Wollard, nor does his name appear in the death records. The writer probably confused him with Otto Roland, who was shot and killed that day while just passing by, as the sheriff put it. The unnamed klansman would have been Dewey Newbold and the Shelton gang member could have been Chester Reid, the brother-in-law of Dr. C.

The Shelton forces drove off to Marion, Ill., spent the night in the sheltering walls of the jail there, and drove on to East St. Louis next day. There was a short truce. But it didn't last long.

Glenn Young Returns

S. Glenn Young, the imported Ku Klux Klan raider and gunman, returned to Herrin a little later. His coming provided new disturbances, and the Herrin business men got together and offered him $1,000 to leave town, because his presence was causing disorder and hurting business. Young turned it down.

The first ripple came when Deputy Sheriff Ora Thomas arrested Young for carrying concealed weapons. Young

S. Glenn Young, who led the klan party in Herrin until he died in a gun battle in a hotel lobby on Jan. 10, 1925.

E. Black. Sheriff Galligan denied Reid had taken part in the fight and was just an innocent bystander. Phemister was in downtown Herrin that day working as the bailiff for the Herrin City Court during the Cagle murder trial. He was also a special deputy sheriff for Galligan despite having been arrested earlier that year with a large quantity of "white mule" and stolen merchandise. [Jan. 18, 1924. "Still More Raids in Williamson Co.." *The Free Press* (Carbondale, Ill.). 1]. On Oct. 18, the county dropped the charges against Phemister after his death. However his brother Thurman Phemister pled guilty that day for possessing intoxicating liquor which had been "found in a barn near the house into which Phemister had only lived a short time." The judge fined him $200. [Oldham Paisley, comp. 2006. *Newspaper Articles from Oldham Paisley's Scrapbooks, Vol. 5 & 6, Klan-Young-Birger*. Marion, Ill.: Williamson County Historical Society. 39-40. Oct. 18, 1924. "Herrin Men Get Sentence."]

produced credentials showing him to be a deputy sheriff in Vermillion Co., and the charge was dropped. But the enmity rankled.

The climax came on the night of Jan. 10, 1925.[12] Thomas was lounging against the cigar counter in the lobby of the European hotel in Herrin. Young entered, with four or five men at his heels. He and Thomas reached for their pistols together.

Thomas was the quicker. Young went down with two bullets in his side. One of his guards was shot down, and Thomas, in his turn, also went down with a bullet in his head.

Young died there in the hotel. Thomas, mortally wounded, was taken to the Herrin hospital. Dr. C. E. Black, head of the hospital, had earned klan hatred by ministering to wounded Shelton gangsters, and armed klansmen broke in that night to avenge Young's death.

Dr. Black fled down a hallway and escaped over the roof. The klansmen crowded into the room where Thomas lay dying, hit is bandaged face savagely and spat in his eyes.

Thomas died that night. Before he died, however, he asked an attendant:

"Did I get Glenn?"

"Yes, you killed him," he was told.

"Well, I'm willing to die, then," he said. And he breathed his last.

Young was buried in a concrete vault on the edge of the Herrin cemetery. Since his death that vault has been a target for pistol shots from countless passing autos. His widow has remarried her late husband's chauffeur, and I understand they are

---

[12] The day is wrong. The shootout took place Jan. 24, 1925.

now running a barbecue stand at Patoka, Ill.

The Sheltons, meanwhile, figured a change of scene would be a good idea, and drove south to Florida. There they began to build up the big rum-running organization that was to make so much money for them during the next 12 months — and cause so many deaths.

Chapter 4

It was shortly before Christmas 1924, that the Shelton brothers finished their survey of the route between the Florida east coast and southern Illinois and put their liquor-running organization into action. The Sheltons made good money in this racket.

They bought their liquor at a Florida inlet, 10 miles south of Daytona, on an f.o.b. system — cargoes weren't paid for until the cars were loaded and ready to leave the dock.

Close Call

This saved Bernie Shelton plenty of money once, when the dry agents swooped down on him just as two cars were being loaded. They confiscated both cars and their contents, and Bernie had to post cash bonds, which, of course, he forfeited; but he hadn't had to pay for the liquor anyway. Altogether, that episode cost him about $13,000.

One of the cars seized in this raid had been disguised as an oil truck, and its confiscation ended a long and useful career. To all outward appearance it was an ordinary oil tank wagon, covered with grime and grease and carrying inside a 110 gallon gas tank which could be drained by spigots in the rear. Thus any motorist stalled along the way could be supplied with gas, and many were. But a panel behind the driver's seat gave access to the main tank's interior where 75 or 80 cases of whisky could be hidden.

Coupes Carried Lots

Coupes were popular rum carriers for a long while, until the dry agents got on to the racket. They were favorites in the trade.

Cavities under the seat and beneath the floor of the rear compartment could hold between 350 and 400 quart bottles.

Sedans were used when the coupes had to be abandoned, with cavities under the floor and eats. Ordinary trucks were also used, with compartments could be carried when the truck was apparently empty.

Their southern "terminal" was this inlet from the Atlantic ocean, just north of New Smyrna, Fla., and about 10 miles south of Daytona. There the autos were loaded with liquor brought in by boat, usually from a base on West End Island, in the Bahamas.

As originally used, the route ran north toward Jacksonville on the Dixie highway. Skirting Jacksonville (they detoured around nearly all the large cities) it hit the Dixie highway again up through Waycross to Ocilla, Ga., went on northwest into Alabama and north on state highway No. 37 to Hefflin. Thence it led west to Aniston, north to Gadsden and up through the mountains on state highway No. 2.

A Division Point

The route entered Tennessee at South Pittsburg and followed federal highway No. 41 northwest to a point a little over 15 miles southeast of Nashville.

Here, at a negro's little plantation near Smyrna, Tenn., was the end of the first day's run. The rum cars were simply driven into a barn and the drivers literally "hit the hay" in the loft — rather rough accommodations, but any bed looked good after that long 500-mile grind.

From that point on the route skirted Nashville, came back to federal highway No. 41 and followed it into Kentucky, reaching a garage about 20 miles south of Henderson and the Ohio river as the end of the second day's run. The garage also served as a remount station and carried a large stock of tires, spare parts and so on. The rum cars were run into it and left there over night. To be sure, the boys who ran the garage would help themselves to a case once in a while — but no one objected to it. They were good fellows.

Men Escort Cars

At this garage the cars were met by escorts for the trip through southern Indiana and Illinois. "Tails," these escorts were called. They were touring cars, and well-armed men in them, and they would follow the rum cars at a close distance, both to guard against hi-jackers and prohibition agents. If the agents chased the rum cars these "tails" would get across the road and block pursuit. They carried no liquor and so were relatively safe even if pinched.

The main booze highway then leads up through Henderson, across the Ohio by ferry and into Indiana. Skirting Evansville, it goes north to Princeton, Ind., and then west to the Mt. Carmel ferry across the Wabash river. Indiana's a "hot state" — liquor law violators get stiff sentences — so the run across it is made as short as possible.

Georgia Gets "Hot"

At Mt. Carmel the route splits. The Chicago whisky runners go north on Illinois state highway No. 1; the Shelton route led west on highway No. 15 into East St. Louis, or down into Williamson county, as the occasion required.

That, roughly, was the original route. In the spring of 1925, however, Georgia got to be a "hot" state and protection was shut off for everybody except one big bootlegger. So the southern part of the route was altered to keep clear of Georgia.

The purchase money was always sent to Florida by telegraph, to avoid the possibility of robbery en route. Carl Shelton generally handled the selling end up north, Earl handled the money in Florida and Bernie and Charley Briggs did most of the hauling.

American Whisky

At first they handled American whisky exclusive — stuff that had been exported from this county and reshipped back to its clearance port. This ran out in May 1925 and from then on they fell back on Canadian and foreign brands. Old Dominion, Rill's Irish, Canadian Club and Burke's Irish Moss were the most popular. This stuff sold at the dock for about $31 a case and sold up north anywhere between $75 and $85 a case.

Thus, on a trip that took only four or five days, they could clean up a net profit from $1000 to $1500. So of course, they got rich.

In the middle of 1925 they decided to change the southern terminal of their route to New Orleans, where one of their St. Louis friends was getting the trade cornered.

Chapter 5

It was in the spring of 1925 that the Sheltons shifted the base of their rum-running activities from Florida to New Orleans. Ray Stephenson, a St. Louis gambler and a close friend of theirs, had established himself in the liquor smuggling business at New Orleans, and the Sheltons naturally teamed up with him. The stuff came in by boat and was brought north by auto, on a route leading through Jackson, Miss., Memphis, Tenn., then over to Arkansas and up through Missouri, striking into Illinois again at Cairo.

Stephenson was sitting pretty. But an accident ended things for him; he fell from his boat during a storm in the gulf on day and was drowned before they could reach him.

An Important Customer

But he isn't as important in this story as a wholesale whisky customer we then had in Harrisburg, Ill. — a little, wiry chap named Charlie Birger.

I guess if the Sheltons had known then what they know now, they would have put a few bullets in Birger's head the first time they sold him a case of booze. It would have been better for everybody if they had. But Birger was just a customer then; they couldn't know that he was to be the bitterest, most deadly enemy they would ever have. Birger is about 46 now. Born at Gainsainy, Russia, of Jewish parents, he had been brought up in St. Louis, living by his wits and selling papers until out of his 'teens. When he was 20 he joined the U.S. cavalry.[13]

---

[13] Birger's older sister placed his birth at Kovno, Russia, which is now Kaunas, Lithuania.

Birger as a boy sold papers in St. Louis
1
Fell from horse while in army and now draws pension
2
CHARLIE BIRGER
Became one of the Sheltons' best wholesale bootleg customers
3
4
Opened saloon in Southern Illinois in 1915

Taught Him to Shoot

It's a funny thing; they say, "Join the army and learn a trade." That's just what Birger did. He became an expert pistol shot while in the army; and that stood him in good stead years later. If the army hadn't taught him to shoot he might have been dead long before now.

Another thing; Birger is drawing a pension right now from the U.S. government. Here is a man who is classed as "one-fourth disabled" by the government in awarding him a $15-a-month pension and yet he is able to lead one of the most desperate gangs in recent years and carry on a very thriving bootleg business.

Birger was in the army from July 5, 1901 to July 4, 1904. One day he fell from a horse, suffering a slight contusion of the right hip. His ring finger on the left hand has been amputated and in 1921 government doctors found Birger had some slight lung trouble, chronic bronchitis and rheumatism.

About 1915 Birger came into southern Illinois, where he set up in business as a saloon keeper. Soon afterward, while operating a place at Ledford, Ill., Charlie's pistol won the right to its first notch — had the out-of-date practice of notching guns prevailed in southern Illinois. A quarrelsome drinker had drawn a gun on a constable friend of Charlie's in the latter's saloon one night and was threatening to fire when Charlie's gun leaped out and put an abrupt stop to his threats.

Bartender Killed

Birger operated other places in and around Harrisburg, Ill., until after the World War, when he extended his activities to Williamson county, adjoining his home county, Saline. He set up the Half Way House, between Marion and Herrin, Ill., and there, in 1922, another figurative notch was added to Charlie's pistol. A young bartender of Birger's had been paying too ardent attentions to one of his employer's many women friends and crumpled up with a pistol ball through the heart while engaged in lacing his shoes one morning. There were no witnesses to the killing and no charges were ever lodged against Birger.[14]

Meanwhile Birger had married and was waxing prosperous. Then in 1923 federal authorities nabbed him on a bootlegging charge. While this charge was still pending, another killing occurred in Birger's place, that of Whitey Doering, a well-known St. Louis gangster who belonged to the Egan's Rats "Mob."[15]

Doering and Birger had engaged in a heated argument over attentions Whitey charged Birger way paying to his, Whitey's girl. Whitey finally screamed a threat that he would kill Birger and, drawing a pistol, fired twice. Both shots went wild and before he cold press the trigger again a lieutenant of Birger's had dropped him to the floor with a well-placed bullet — dead.

Self-Defense Plea Wins

Birger was credited with the killing in the coroner's investigation that followed but was exonerated by the coroner's jury on grounds of self-defense.

Then came Birger's trial on the federal charge of bootlegging and his sentence to a year in jail at Danville, Ill., where, with the aid of $700, according to his own story, he promptly became a trusty.

Then, while Charlie was still in jail, early in 1924, his wife

---

[14] The bartender was Cecil Knighton. Other accounts list it as a shootout that took place Nov. 14, 1923.

[15] The shootout with Doering followed on Nov. 18.

disappeared with another chap, leaving their two youngsters behind. Half Way House fell victim to the kluxers' torch during Birger's enforced absence, also, so that when he was freed at the end of seven months he was poorer in several respects than when he was jailed.

In addition to that Birger lived in fear that Egan's Rats would exact vengeance for Whitey's death. For the latter reason, Birger put one John Davis, or Hoghead, as he was better known, a lieutenant who had been watching over Charlie's interests while the latter was in jail, on his payroll as his personal bodyguard.

Birger's precautions were unnecessary, though, for Dinty Colbeck, known as leader of the Rats, had decided that his followers would keep their hands off the affair, as Doering's killing had resulted only from an argument over a woman.

Starts Over Again

It was tough sailing for Birger for a while after he got out of jail. He still had three farms of about 300 acres near Harrisburg that he had invested some of his earlier booze profits in, his comfortable cottage on the western outskirts of Harrisburg and some business property on an adjoining lot but as far as ready cash was concerned he was practically broke.

He set up headquarters at Harrisburg and resumed bootlegging but on a far smaller scale than formerly, Hoghead Davis was given a residence of one of Birger's farms, five mile west of Harrisburg, and home-made liquor was supplied from there. Birger's lack of capital forced him to cater to small customers, to whom he made deliveries in gallon lots at first. He gradually built up his cash capital again, but in January of 1925, lost the services of his lieutenant, Hoghead.

Chapter 6

A pool room scuffle in Harrisburg, Ill., in which a young bystander was shot and killed, robbed Birger of the services of his chief lieutenant, Hoghead Davis, early in January, 1925, just as Birger was getting his booze business back on a paying basis following his stay in jail on a federal bootlegging charge.[16]

Three hours after the killing Davis was furnished an auto and spirited out of Saline county, leaving his two children (he and his wife had separated) in Birger's care. The latter kept the youngsters for about a month, then placed them in an orphan asylum. Authorities are still looking for Davis.

Birger employed other helpers and continued in the rum game, among them being Arb Treadway, Art Newman, Freddy Wooten, Ward "Casey" Jones, William "Hi-Pockets" McQuay and one "Alabam" — all of whom were to figure more or less prominently in later developments.[17]

Treadway, who served until his death as Birger's chief lieutenant, was a wild and daring chap of 27, who claimed Paragould, Ark., as his home. He was a good dresser, thin-faced, pallid and clean-shaven, and quarrelsome when drunk.

A Devoted Husband

Newman, 33, who is still alive and Birger's chief aide, formerly operated a hotel in East St. Louis. He was practically ruined financially as a result of his arrest, trial and acquittal in connection

---

[16] Johnson is off by a week or so. The incident took place on either Christmas Eve or the day after Christmas depending the source. All the sources, including the death certificate, agree that Davis' victim finally succumbed to his wounds Dec. 26, 1924.

[17] "Alabam" was Alabama-born Riley Simmons.

with the murder of one Charley Gardner in a saloon operated by the Shelton boys in East St. Louis. Wooten, a former bartender at Newman's hotel and who was held in connection with the Gardner killing for a time, is about 26 and, incidentally, a devoted husband and father.

Jones was an ex-convict from a southern prison who came into southern Illinois from Kentucky. "Hi-Pockets" McQuay was recruited from amongst the hangers-on in the liquor business around Herrin.

In the spring of 1925 Birger decided that Williamson county was a safer site for his activities than Saline and established a tourist camp and barbecue stand about 12 miles west of Harrisburg as his headquarters — Shady Rest, he called the place.

"The Cabin" Dynamited

Birger was not in the case lot class in the booze business and was wholesaling to various road-houses in Williamson county. In the fall he decided to build "The Cabin" at Shady Rest. This building was of rustic structure, built from logs felled on the premises.

It was this building that recently was dynamited, causing the deaths of four persons.

Birger invested about $10,000 in Shady Rest, where in addition to the other attractions he had a small menagerie, a dog and chicken fighting pit, a bar, a bottling establishment and gambling tables.

Meanwhile, Birger continued to prosper in the booze business, getting much of his better stuff through the Sheltons. He followed a policy of cutting this before wholesaling it, so that by the time it reached the consumer only about one-fifth of the original contents of a quart remained — a proportion which holds good in practically every quart of "good imported stuff" sold today.

Such "cutting" was skillfully done. A St. Louis house supplied bottles (both of the "non-refillable" and other types), caps and labels at $3 a case, though $5 was the usual price to the trade. Counterfeit seals were readily obtained.

Slot Machines

In November of 1925 Birger suggested to the Shelton boys that they combine forces and gain control of the slot machines rights (a highly lucrative concession) in Williamson county and install the contrivances in some of the many roadhouses there.

The Sheltons agreed, with the understanding that Birger would furnish the bulk of the capital while the Sheltons were to secure the required protection from the authorities.

So on Dec. 18 all the machines held previously by the Sheltons and Birger were consolidated and I was employed to attend to collections at $30 a week and expenses.

In the succeeding month the score or so of machines returned a net profit of $867, or half the receipts. The other half went to the various roadhouse owners in whose places they were kept.

Then on Feb. 13, 1926, a shut-down order came from the state's attorney's office at Marion and the places were closed, but for a short time only. On their reopening Birger decided my expenses were running too high and gave one John Howard my job at $100 a month and expenses.

Real Cause of Feud

In the first five weeks under Howard's administration the machines returned a net profit of $1700, which was turned over to

Birger in his capacity of treasurer of the business. Charlie called Carl Shelton in, this was in March, 1926, and gave him $300 as the Sheltons' share.

Unfortunately for Birger he fired Howard and replaced him with "Casey" Jones. Howard then told Carl just how much the Sheltons' agreed 50-50 split should have been and there you have the real cause of the Birger-Shelton feud.[18]

Birger held out $550 on the Sheltons and the result was the bloodiest gang warfare in American history. The community has been terrified through the frequent use of machine guns, aerial bombs and dynamite and many men have been killed.

Even Birger Doesn't Know

Birger is still under the delusion that it was caused by the Sheltons' suspicion that he pocketed $1000 which a Harrisburg garage man had offered for the recovery of a diamond ring taken from him in a robbery staged by some gangsters.

The Sheltons, despite their discovery of the double-crossing, decided to bide their time for a while.

Meanwhile, over in Herrin, klan and anti-klan hatred was being kept alive. On April 13, 1926, his hatred burst forth into a fresh lame of spitting guns.

---

[18] Howard died later that year on Aug. 16, 1926, shot outside a pool room in the small mining community of Harco, in western Saline Co., Illinois.

Chapter 7

Williamson county was running in its usual wide open-state as the spring of 1926 drew on. Early in March Bernie Shelton had quit driving booze cars up from Florida and had opened a road house just north of Herrin.

All the Sheltons' extensive Williamson county whisky business was now being directed from Bernie's place. This business was of a wholesale nature mostly, supplying the dozens of road-houses in the county. It was all jake with the county authorities, who were collecting from $15 to $35 a week from each roadhouse, depending upon the amount of business each did.

Steel Garage Loft

Then John Smith at whose garage seven men were killed in a pitched battle nearly two years before, came back to Herrin from a well-advised vacation trip down into Kentucky. Smith, after that battle built a steel, window-less room into the loft of his garage, and he is reputed to have retreated into this shelter and stayed there for nearly three months without as much as venturing forth for his raids.

"Well, you fellows have been playing around long enough," Smith said to a kluxer, told Floyd 'Jar Down' Arms, one of the Sheltons' followers, shortly after he returned. "The first time you come around and start any trouble you can expect trouble back."

Jar Down reported the conversation at Bernie Shelton's place. The boys out there decided to let things ride for awhile until Carl could come down from East St. Louis for a conference.

Then, shortly before the Herrin city election on April 13,

rumors began to hit of klux plots to elect its entire slate of candidates.

Carl had arrived in Herrin and steps were taken by anti-klan forces, among which were Sheriff Galligan and Shelton and Birger and their followers, to prevent any "irregularities at the polls" as they expressed.

A force of 15 men were gathered at Bernie's place on the night of April 12, armed with Thompson submachine guns, shotguns, rifles and pistols, and held in readiness for any emergency. In this way, they planned to prevent irregularities.

A Sweet Smelling Gangster

Election day dawned with everyone looking for trouble. Jovial "Blacky" Arms sprayed himself with pungent perfume as the gangsters looked over their weapons that morning.

"If I die today, I want to go to my grave smelling good," he joked.

Hostilities were not long in developing. John Smith challenged two Italian voters at the polls and a car bristling with arms and carrying Blacky, Ray Walker and others dashed into Herrin. Smith was disarmed, given a beating and warned that further trouble would mean his death.

Smith was removed as an election official and went back to his garage.

The anti-klan car roamed the streets for a while, its occupants finally concluding that Smith might as well be bumped off. Accordingly, its course was directed past Smith's garage.

As it whizzed past, "Blacky" fired directly as Smith, who chanced to be standing in front of his business place. The bullet scorched the kluxer's neck. It was trouble from then on.

HERRIN AT THE POLLS

In less than an hour the anti-klan forces were concentrated in Herrin and storming Smith's place with machine gun, rifle and revolver fire.

Smith and his two employees barricaded themselves in the steel room and, as they failed to return the fire, and anti-klan forces finally withdrew with no casualties on either side.

The respite was brief, however.

Toward dusk Carl Shelton spotted John Ford, treasurer of Williamson county and considered a kluxer, walking down the street toward the polling place in the Masonic Temple. Shelton waved his motor cavalcade to the curb where a hurried conference was held and a decision reached to get Ford.

Birger in Lead

Charlie Birger piloted the lead car as the gangsters' caravan roared down upon Ford, who was just entering the polling place, opposite the Herrin hospital.

Arb Treadway, Birger's chief lieutenant, sprang to the sidewalk as the leader's car drew abreast of Ford and at the point of a pistol commanded the latter to throw up his hands. The three other cars drew up behind. Noble Weaver leaped out behind Treadway, menacing Ford anew.

Then, before the kluxer could respond to Treadway's command spitting flame burst from two cars which stood, curtained and previously unnoticed, across the street in front of the hospital.

Treadway dropped mortally wounded, a bullet boring through his body just above the heart and another through his abdomen. An instant later Weaver fell to the sidewalk as a ball pierced his head. The anti-kluxers had run smack into an ambush!

Rattling volleys of shotgun and rifle fire continued from the curtained cars across the street as the gangsters tumbled from their cars with a machine gun and pistols at the ready and loosed a staccato return. Charley Briggs, Shelton aide, slumped dead in his seat in the second car.

Machine Gun Jams

But the jinx still stayed with the gangsters. Suddenly, as they poured their fire into the enemy's autos from behind the shelter of their own cars, their machine gun jammed. Odds were now against them, and with rifle and shotgun charges boring their ranks, they hurriedly quit the field of battle, leaving their dead and wounded behind. Treadway and Weaver were carried into the hospital, where they died a few hours later.

Three kluxers had fallen, too — Harland Ford, a brother of John Ford, and two brothers, Sizemore by name.[19] Two of the three fell victims to the machine gun's bullets before it jammed — there might have been a far different story to tell had that not happened — and one of the gangsters' pistol bullets had claimed the life of the third.

That was the last time that Birger and the Shelton boys were ever comrades in arms. Events moved swiftly now to the launching of warfare between the two gangs.

---

[19] The two brothers were J. E "Ben" and William MacFerson "Mack" Sizemore. The former worked as a coal miner. The latter served as a Herrin alderman.

Chapter 8

The Sheltons were still nursing their secret grudge against Charlie Birger for his wrongful division of the slot machine spoils and they now decided to drop all pretence of friendliness with the increasingly powerful little booze baron for Harrisburg.

Birger by this time had added a new line to his whisky racket — the sale of doctored near beer.

Inasmuch as Birger had been buying whisky from the Sheltons, he now assumed that the Sheltons would buy his new beer goods in return and accordingly sent ten cases over to the Sheltons' roadhouse north of Herrin.

Partly because of the Shelton's secret grudge and partly because the beer was not up to standard, Bernie Shelton returned it.[20] Then Birger came to Carl Shelton, still believing they were on good terms, and told him that he (Birger) had lost two pistols and several rifles in the election day battle. "Blacky" Arms, one of the Sheltons' followers, was carrying one of the lost pistols, Birger said. He requested its return.

Shut Off Birger's Supply

The pistol was never returned and Carl never gave a reason for allowing Arms to retain it.

Those circumstances forced Birger to sense that an ill feeling existed — a feeling that was strengthened late in May when the

---

[20] While other contemporary accounts mention Birger's bottling operations, Johnson's account is the only one that referred to the Sheltons rejection of Birger's beer. A mid-September 1926 news story dated the split between the gangs as "a few months ago." It also noted that since the split "several affrays have occurred and reports of members of one faction having hi-jacked automobile cargoes of liquor of the other have reached county officials." [Sept. 13, 1926. "Herrin Again Kills, Robs." *The Free Press* (Carbondale, Ill.). 1].

Sheltons refused to sell him any more of the liquor they had been running up from Florida.

As ill feeling grew between the Shelton boys and Birger, the rum runners and hangers-on in the Williamson county liquor traffic began to align themselves with the opposing camps.

County Wide Open

The county was running wide open again as usual, following a few weeks of restrictions placed into effect when National Guard troops were brought into the county after the election day battle at Herrin.

Chief among the frequenters of Birger's Shady Rest resort as battle lines were forming for the gang warfare were Ward "Casey" Jones, Art Newman, Freddy Wooten, Connie Ritter and one "Alabam." Over at the Sheltons' place, north of Herrin, "Blacky" and "Jar Down" Arms, Ray and Harry Walker, "Wild Bill" Holland, Everett Schmidt, "Oklahoma Curly" Hardin and Max "Pat" Pulliam held forth.[21]

"Hi-Pockets" McQuay continued friendly with both sides for a time and stories he carried to Birger from the Shelton camp finally placed Birger on his guard.

The Break

Then, in July, Birger and Carl Shelton came face to face at Shaw's Garden, a roadhouse between Johnston City and West Frankfort in which Birger was interested.

---

[21] Pulliam uses both Schmidt and Schmitt for Everett's surname. Other newspapers at the time of the incident used Smith. The correct spelling has not been determined, though his death certificate is in the name of Everett Smith. It's quite possible that he used some of the different spellings as aliases.

Shelton whipped
out his pistol "Charlie
you------, I ought to
kill you" he said

Carl
Shelton

Birger, with four or five men at his heels, walked up to Carl, who was surrounded by an equal force of his own men. [22]

"Carl, what have you got against me?" Birger demanded.

Shelton whipped out his pistol.

"Charlie, you — —, I ought to kill you," he said. But after a few more hot words Carl withdrew with his men.

Birger, after this, quietly began to assemble his forces.

Later in July, "Oklahoma Curly" Hardin was lost to the Shelton forces through the gun of one of Sheltons' own men, Harry Walker.[23]

Wrong Man Held for Murder

"Curly," drunk and quarrelsome, swaggered into Ed Roccassi's resort north of Herrin and asked to see Ed, who was closeted with Walker in a rear room. Roccassi's wife barred Curly's way and received a bullet through the hand from one of the two pistols the Oklahoman habitually carried.

Walker jerked open the door at the sound of the shot and emptied his revolver into Curly's body. Roccassi assumed responsibility for Curly's death, and inasmuch as Curly had wounded Mrs. Roccassi this offered a good defense. He is free on bond now, with the case still pending.

The Sheltons lost two more men a few days later when Harry

---

[22] Birger gangster Harvey Dungey may have referred to this incident in one of his drawings. In Drawing #29, he shows a similar scene except generally referred with Shelton holding a .45 at Birger and latter begging for his life telling Carl to remember that he had three daughters. Dungey, whose accuracy and credibility was notoriously bad, also dated the incident to October 1926. Since August 2009, copies of some of Dungey's drawings, have been on display at the Franklin County Jail Museum in Benton.

[23] This incident took place on Monday, July 12, 1926. Hardin was known to his local girlfriend as Boyd Hartin (as the paper reported), Howard E. Johnson at Herrin Hospital and John Franklin Armstrong to his family. He was the first person to be identified in Williamson County by the use of fingerprints.

Walker himself and Everett Schmidt were killed in a gun fight at Ted's Place, a roadhouse north of Marion.[24] A coroner's jury returned a verdict that they had shot each other, but inasmuch as they were the best of friends it is the general opinion in gangland that they were killed by a third person as the result of the increasing friction between the Birger and Shelton gangs.

Then Open Warfare

Threats and counter-threats filtered back and forth between the two camps until late in September. Then open warfare burst out.

One night as "Wild Bill" Holland of the Shelton forces, with Pat Pulliam and his wife, emerged from Gene's Place, a roadhouse between Marion and Herrin, and seated themselves in Pulliam's auto, fire from machine guns was opened up on it.[25]

Holland slumped in his seat, instantly killed by the 14 bullets that bit into his body. Mr. and Mrs. Pulliam were wounded.

---

[24] Walker and Schmitt's death took place Aug. 22, 1926.

[25] Other sources give the name of the roadhouse as Grover's Place. This incident took place on Sept. 12, 1926.

Chapter 9

The Sheltons now fitted up an armored truck for forays into Birger's territory. Bullet-proof vests were worn by members of both gangs. Fresh supplies of ammunition and additional machine guns for and small arms were secured.

Then in October, 1926, the Sheltons launched their first offensive — a machine gun attack on Birger's log cabin and barbecue stand headquarters at Shady Rest, 12 miles west of Harrisburg.[26]

Six men, armed to the teeth and riding in Shelton's armored truck, participated in the attack. Machine gun fire was poured into the roadside barbecue stand as the armored truck swept by.

No casualties resulted, though the place was perforated with bullets.

No Chivalry

As luck would have it (for the Sheltons), their armored truck met Art Newman, Birger's chief aide, coming westward out of Harrisburg, his wife seated in his car beside him. Chivalry holds no place in gangland's code, and the machine gun was turned full on Newman's car as the armored truck swept by. Newman almost miraculously escaped injury, but his wife was wounded in the leg and his car was wrecked by the hail of .45 caliber slugs.

The Sheltons swept their truck around and fled back westward toward Marion, expecting a hot pursuit from Birger and his men. North of Marion they drew in between two roadhouses,

---

[26] The Sheltons debuted their armored car in the attacks on Monday, Oct. 4, 1926.

Here is "The Cabin" at Shady Rest, built by Charlie Birger, and recently dynamited, causing the deaths of four persons. During the gang warfare, Birger generally had the "lieutenant" at the left on guard on the porch with a machine gun. *The Sheboygan Press*, Jan. 22, 1925.

got the machine guns ready, and in this ambush they waited for the expected pursuit.

After More Recruits

Disappointed in this, they drove on to Shaw's Garden, a roadhouse between Johnson City and West Frankfort, in which Birger was interested, and accorded it attentions similar to those they had just showered on Birger's barbecue stand.

After this foray the Sheltons retreated to East St. Louis to secure additional recruits for new battles. These recruits were mostly enlisted from the ranks of the notorious Cuckoo gang and other groups of thugs and gunmen in St. Louis and East St. Louis.

Birger, meanwhile, had not been idle. On Oct. 13, he and his men descended on the Sheltons' roadhouse, north of Herrin, in an improved armored car and wrecked the resort. This brought the Sheltons back post haste, with a choice collection of St. Louis toughs at their heels.

Their forces now numbered about 29, as against about 25 that Birger had recruited from among his friends in and around Harrisburg and nearby mining communities. Ten or more autos were at the disposal of both gangs.

Snipers

For three or four days after their return the Sheltons maintained an armed guard behind the concrete coping of a roadhouse adjoining the one Birger had wrecked, waiting to snipe off any of the Birgerites that might appear to finish the work of destruction. The wily Birger was not to be caught thus, however.

The Sheltons now moved their headquarters to West City, Ill., where they were on friendly business terms with Joe Adams, the late and corpulent mayor of that village. From this headquarters they launched a fresh excursions against Shaw's Garden and burned it to the ground, but Birger had already abandoned the place.[27]

Dynamite Trap

After the embers had cooled a new trap was laid for Birger. Four hundred sticks of dynamite were planted in and about the

---

[27] This raid took place on Oct. 28, 1926.

ruins and fused to central points from which wires led to a station 300 feet away from which the mine could be touched off.

For four days two men were kept on guard, waiting for Birger and his men to come and inspect the ruins, but Birger proved too foxy again and never came near his ruined roadhouse.[28]

---

[28] Birger told a similar story himself, except he said the Sheltons placed the dynamite around the burned house where investigators found the body of Lyle "Shag" Worsham after he had been murdered and the body charred by the fire on Sept. 18, 1926. Birger told this story in response questions regarding the assassination of Joe Adams. He also denied any gang connection to Worsham's killing, though three of his men machine-gunned him down on a road south of Carterville, Ill., while Birger and other members of the gang watched. At the time, they thought the man had been reporting back Birger's activities to the Shelton Gang. [Dec. 13, 1926. "Birger Denies Adams Murder." *The Free Press* (Carbondale, Ill.). 1.]

Chapter 10

Two deaths in quick succession marked a new flaring of gangland's civil war about the middle of November, 1926.[29]

"Hi-Pockets" McQuay, the Herrin hanger-on, who by this time had become definitely aligned with Birger, was found dead in his bullet perforated car on a road between Herrin and Johnston City early one morning.

A day later a small boy noticed a human hand sticking stiffly above the surface of a creek that ran beneath a highway bridge near Equality. Authorities found the body of Ward "Casey" Jones, punctured by six bullets and wrapped in a blanket. Bloodstains on the bridge floor indicated that his body had been tossed out of an auto.

Bombs From the Air

Next came the aerial bombardment of Birger's cabin — probably the first time in history that an airplane was used by gangster against gangster.[30]

The dynamite sticks that had been planted in the ruins of Shaw's Garden, Birger's other roadhouse, by the Sheltons in a vain effort to blow up Birger were retrieved and fashioned into crude bombs after an unsuccessful attempt had been made to get St. Louis blackhanders to fashion engines of destruction.[31] Three

---

[29] Both bodies were found not in November, but on Oct. 26, 1926.

[30] The aerial attack took place on Nov. 12, 1926.

[31] "Blackhanders" refer to members of the Black Hand, a Sicilian precursor to the mafia that specialized in extortion rackets. They frequently used bombs to make their point. Because they didn't organize in large groups and used anonymous letters, they were often imitated by non-Sicilian gangsters.

bombs, each composed of 12 sticks of dynamite wired around a half-pint bottle of nitroglycerine, were loaded into a privately owned plane. Ray Walker took the pilot's seat and "Jar Down" Arms the observer's.[32]

Two bombs were released as the plane soared over Birger's cabin at an altitude of about 500 feet. Birger's men had run out at the sound of the plane's motor, but held their fire until after the bombs had fallen, fearing it was a government plane.

They turned loose their guns furiously but vainly when the plane swooped back over and dropped the third bomb, however. The returned aviators reported that one of the bombs exploded but Birger has declared that all three were duds.

Sheltons Arrested by U.S.

Before other hostilities could occur Carl and Bernie Shelton were taken into custody at West City and charged with the Collinsville mail robbery, in which a $15,000 mine payroll had been lost back in November, 1924.[33]

Two postal inspectors, six deputy United States marshals and a Franklin county deputy sheriff surrounded the homes of Gus and Joe Adams, where the Sheltons were, and made the arrests, the boys surrendering peaceable. Earl Shelton was arrested in Fairmont City soon afterward.

They were held under $60,000 bonds each, which only Earl has

---

[32] If Johnson's account is true at this point, then where did the pilot sit? Unless one of the gangsters doubled as a wing walker, the pilot, 26-year-old Elmer Kane would have had to occupy one of the two seats in the plane. Many later accounts list Monroe "Blackie" Armes as the second man in the plane which is another impossibility as he had already reported to Leavenworth for stealing a car by this date. Since Armes is recalled in other stories, the second man may have been his brother Floyd "Jar Down" Armes rather than Walker.

[33] Authorities arrested the Sheltons shortly after the plane took off from West City to bomb Shady Rest. The mail robbery took place not in November 1924, but the morning of Jan. 27, 1925.

succeeded in raising at this writing. The other two are still in jail, awaiting trial on January 31, in federal court at Springfield.[34]

Mayor Adams Killed

Mayor Joe Adams, friend of the Sheltons, was the victim of the next burst of fire from gangster guns. His death came on December 12, soon after the Sheltons' arrest. Two men called at Adams' home, telling Mrs. Adams they had a letter from Carl Shelton that must be delivered to Adams personally.

Mrs. Adams awakened her husband from a nap and he went to the door unsuspectingly. As he reached for the letter, three shots rang out from pistols his callers had concealed in their pockets.

Adams' huge bulk — he weighed 300 pounds — toppled to the floor, a bullet hole above his heart, one below it and another in his head. Adams lived just long enough to say that he recognized neither of his assailants, who had fled to a waiting car as their victim fell.

The letter, which had fluttered to the floor as Adams was shot, said merely that here were two boys out of work and if Adams could use them it would be appreciated. It was signed "C. S."

Quits the Gang

The coroner's jury returned an open verdict during the interval that Adams' huge body lay waiting the arrival of a special casket from St. Louis in which burial could be made. Birger has since been sought on a warrant charging him with connection

---

[34] A jury convicted the brothers on Feb. 4, 1927, and the judge sentenced them to 25 years at Leavenworth. The judge released them just over three months later to allow for a new trial after a key witness, a member of the Birger Gang, admitted that he had perjured himself on the stand.

with the killing.

On December 14, Birger and several of his men made a "business trip" to East St. Louis, stopping at DuQuoin and other way points to make inquiries concerning the whereabouts of Carl Shelton and some of his followers. He seemed particularly interested in my whereabouts, I learned the next day when I chanced to stop at DuQuoin. Inasmuch as the Shelton forces had scattered with their leaders' arrest, I decided that so far as I was concerned Birger could have such honors as the situation afforded.

There was no money being made in the booze racket anymore and I'd heard threats that I would be killed if the enemy gangsters ever caught me in Williamson county again. It was just a case of everything to lose and nothing to gain, so I turned my back on the gangland "war zone," through with it forever, I hope.

Chapter 11

So Who Was Ralph Johnson?

By Jon Musgrave

Ralph Johnson may have written 10 installments to his story, but he never actually told his readers his identity. He also never associated any person with a crime unless they were dead, already convicted and in jail, or at least indicted and waiting for trial. Even in the assassination of Caesar Cagle for which Carl and Earl Shelton had been indicted and all believed they were responsible, Johnson made certain he didn't actually name the killers, just how they did it. That was important. The jury didn't acquit the Sheltons of the crime, the state's attorney just withdrew the case when the chief witness decided to be somewhere else than court that day. No statutes of limitation protected the murderers. Had he identified the Sheltons as the killers, as opposed to simply writing about their obvious motive, then he would have made himself a witness to be targeted by a state's attorney, and worse, a target for a hit on himself by the Sheltons and their remaining allies. It's that list of remaining allies that actually help uncover Johnson's real identity.

It's also important to remember that even though the public did not know Johnson's real identify, there's no chance that the Sheltons could be so clueless. They knew him by both his real name and his aliases, and certainly knew the identity of the first man who ran their slot machine partnership.

With the exception of the mysterious Mr. Blackburn that Johnson mentioned from the first Smith Garage shootout, and

"Oklahoma Curley" involved in the Roccassi shooting, all of the other Shelton Gang members had been publicly identified in the papers multiple times based on their arrests and other incidents. Curley had been mentioned as well following the Roccassi shooting, but never identified as a member of the gang.

The shrinking number of Shelton gangsters still living at the time of the "Secrets" publication proved to be Johnson's biggest problem at keeping his identity secret. Top lieutenants like Jack Skelcher, Charlie Briggs, Everett Schmitt (or Smith) and Harry Walker had already died. Others like Monroe "Blackie" Armes and the Shelton Brothers couldn't be Johnson either as they already sat in prison or awaited their own upcoming trials.

STRIKE A POSE — Shadows purposely hide Ralph Johnson's face in this photo sent out to promote the original series of articles. The poor quality represents the microfilmed source.

Former Shelton gangsters Art Newman and Freddy Wooten didn't make likely candidates either for the writer behind the alias. While "Johnson" sold his story to the *St. Louis Star*, Newman negotiated to sell his to the *St. Louis Post-Dispatch*. Both men had also hid out from the Sheltons for most of 1925 and 1926 until they joined Birger's gang. Newman himself told the *Post-Dispatch* that he had been in Miami for the hurricane, which kept in Florida until at least mid September 1926 when the devastating storm struck, and out of the way for the slot machine partnership, the Election Day Riot and the summer shootings of 1926. As for Wooten, it would be extremely odd for him to be Johnson after Johnson's praise of him as a good family man.

That pretty much leaves Ray Walker, Floyd "Jar-Down" Armes and Max "Pat" Pulliam. Walker doesn't fit as a suspect since he stayed loyal to the Sheltons even long after most of the brothers had been shot and killed. He was there when Carl Shelton was killed in 1947, and later supposedly married Bernie Shelton's widow in the decades following his death.

Floyd Armes remains a possibility, but like Walker, his brothers stayed loyal and active in the gang well into the 30s and even possibly the 1940s, though his two younger brothers, Ray "Lefty" and Roy "Tony" Armes, weren't old enough to take part in the exploits of the 1920s. The latter died outside the Green Lantern tavern in Herrin in 1950 after being shot by a sniper, similar fashion to the assassinations of the Shetlons during that same period of 1947 to 1950.[35]

That leaves Max "Pat" Pulliam the last and best choice. Johnson provided a few clues to his true identity. "I got married a year or so ago, and ever since the little woman's been after me to quit the racket. So I have," he claimed in the first installment of the series. Pulliam was 28 at the time Johnson's articles came out. His young wife Mildred claimed to be either 18 or 19.[36]

---

[35] Check out Taylor Pensoneau's books, *Brothers Notorious*, for more on the deaths of the Shelton Brothers by Harris, as well as *Dapper & Deadly*, a biography of Harris himself. An upcoming book by IllinoisHistory.com scheduled for 2011, *Inside the Shelton Gang: A Daughter's Discovery*, by Ruthie Shelton, will tell the story from the view inside the family.

[36] At least that's what newspapers reported in March 1927. Seven months earlier during

What Johnson wrote about Max Pulliam — almost nothing provides another piece of the circumstantial evidence. How Pulliam's mother saved his life in the ambulance a few days after Birger's men killed William "Wild Bill" Holland and injured both Pulliam and his wife represents one of the most colorful stories of the Gang War. It has intrigue, a car chase involving an ambulance and a viscous physical attack stopped only when Mama Pulliam placed her body between her injured helpless son and Charlie Birger himself. For many young men it's macho to be a gangster. It's not to be a mama's boy who has to hide behind his mother's skirts to avoid a whuppin'. It's not a positive piece of evidence, but more of a negative one. The absence of the ambulance story suggests it injured Johnson's pride to the extent that he didn't see any reason to bring it up.

But his occupation proves the best piece of circumstantial evidence. While almost everyone else worked in a coal mine or other hard physical labor before joining the gang, Pulliam was white collar both before and after his gang association. While he had worked as a salesman for different outfits, he'd also tried his hand at writing. In early 1930 at a time he tried to get paroled out of Leavenworth, his father noted, "Max has shown some ability in the past as a writer," possibly referring to the "Secrets" series. At the same time, Carl Choisser, publisher of the *Benton Evening News* offered to give him a job as a writer if he could get paroled.[37] While he didn't get paroled at that point, when he did get out, only one news agency contacted the prison to find out his status — the *St. Louis Star* — Ralph Johnson's old employer. They sent

Birger's attacks against Pulliam, the papers aged her at 22.

[37] Fred C. Pulliam. Jan. 5, 1930. Letter to U.S. Board of Pardons & Parole. Max Pulliam (#32504) Inmate File. Leavenworth Penitentiary Records. National Archives, Kansas City, Mo.

two telegrams wanting to know his whereabouts. The warden responded with the date of Pulliam's release. As to his present whereabouts he had no information.[38] It's unknown if Pulliam ever worked for certain for the *Benton Evening News,* but he definitely reported for the *Belleville News-Democrat* in 1945 across the river from St. Louis. He also claimed to have written for the *Indianapolis Star* as well as a wire service in Chicago. Johnson knew how to tell a story. Pulliam definitely knew how to write.

But the best clue of all proves to be his own words. As to the slot machines, Johnson just claimed to be the collector. Pulliam though claimed a much larger role with the slots and the split between the gangs. Two years after the gang war ended a U.S. attorney declared, "that Pulliam was the owner of the slot machines in Williamson county, Ill., over which the gang trouble originally started." A week later he went further, noting Pulliam claimed to have been "shot by Birger Gangsters in war over slot machines which he owned." Decades later, Pulliam would look back and describe his role in the Shelton Gang as "business manager."[39]

---

[38] Max Pulliam Inmate File. St. Louis Star. July 1, 1931. Telegram to F. G. Zerbst, Warden; St. Louis Star. July 1, 1931. Telegraph to Warden, U.S. Penitentiary; and F. G. Zerbst, Warden. July 2, 1931. Telegram to St. Louis Star.

[39] Max Pulliam Inmate File. "Parole Report By United States Attorney;" Oldham Paisley. 2006. *Newspaper Articles From Oldham Paisley's Scrapbooks, Volume 9, Birger-Boswell-Ritter.* Marion, Ill.: Williamson County Historical Society. May 29, 1929. "Given Two Years on Drug Charges"; and Art Long. Feb. 4, 1958. "Ex-Hoodlum Comes Out of Hiding in Nevada." *Nevada State Journal* (Reno, Nev.). 8.

Chapter 12

So Who's Max Pulliam?

If Max is our man, and I believe he is, then what's his story?

Unlike most followers of the Sheltons and Charlie Birger, Max B. "Pat" Pulliam actually hailed from Southern Illinois born in Franklin County on Dec. 19, 1898, to Fred C. and Nora B. (Browning) Pulliam. Their first and only child, Max entered the world just one year after their marriage on March 17, 1897. In 1900, the family lived in Benton and Pulliam's father worked as the deputy circuit clerk in the courthouse. Ten years later he managed the local brick plant in Benton.[40] His mother, as a Browning, meant that he descended from one of the oldest families in Franklin County and would have been cousins to many of the leading families in the surrounding countryside.

On July 11, 1917, Pulliam enlisted in the Illinois National Guard assigned to Co. F, 4th Regiment at Benton. He registered for the draft on Sept. 12, 1918, at the age of 20. At the time he worked as a brakeman for the Illinois Central Railroad and had a wife named Ruby in Houston, Texas. At this point he signed his name as Max. B. Pulliam. It appears that he served a year during World War I, but whether in the national guard or active service isn't clear. He later claimed one year of military service, and his parents listed him as such in 1930. As to his first wife Ruby, she's never mentioned again.[41]

---

[40] Illinois Statewide Marriage Index, 1763-1900. Illinois State Archives. Secretary of State website; and 1900 and 1910 Censuses of Franklin Co., Illinois. Ancestry.com.

[41] Harry L. Frier, ed. 1920. *Franklin County, Illinois, War History, 1832-1919*. Benton, Ill.: Franklin Co. War History Soc. 121; World War I Draft Registration Cards, 1917-1918, 1930 Censuses of Leavenworth Co., Kan., and Franklin Co., Illinois. Ancestry.com; and Max Pulliam Inmate File.

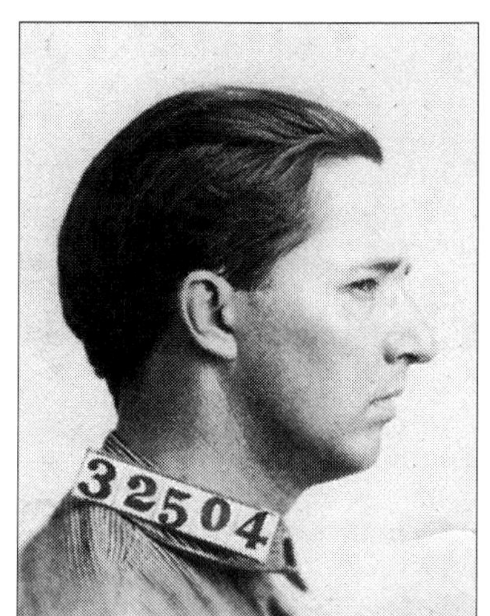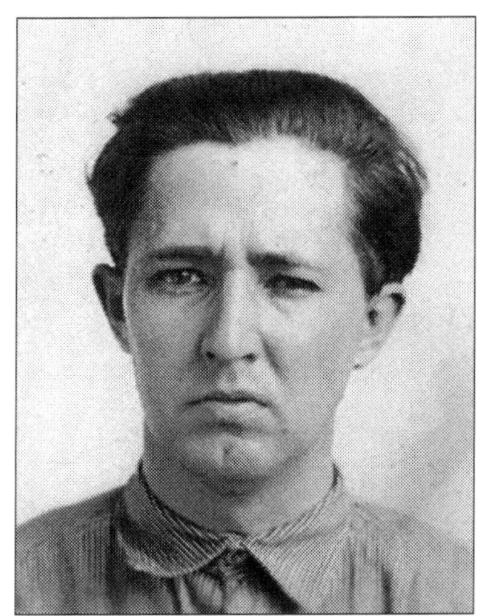

Pulliam's mug shots from May 1929 when he entered Leavenworth.

In 1918 when he registered for the draft the review officer described as tall and slender with blue eyes and light colored hair. A decade later we'd learn just how short tall could be in the second decade of the 20th Century. In 1929, Pulliam would be described as 5' 8 ¾" tall, weight 140 lbs. He suffered from "slightly stooped" posture and only a "fair" general physical condition and teeth. He had a history of gonorrhea and syphilis, used tobacco but didn't drink alcohol. He had taken about 15 grains of narcotics a day since about December 1926. Narcotic scars covered both arms and he had his wife's name "Mildred" tattooed across his chest. Thirty years later in 1958, a reporter in Reno described him as "portly (190 pounds, five feet, nine inches) and neatly dressed. His dark hair is laced with graying streaks. A thin, neatly trimmed mustache reaches from the outside edge of the nostrils down to the corners of his mouth. He wears glasses. His clothing hides his scars."[42]

Pulliam's grandfather Edward A. Pulliam died July 27, 1919, and his grandmother Marie Pulliam moved in with him and his parents around that time. By the 1920 census that January, both Max, who was listed as single again, and his father both worked as commercial salesman for flour. Max, his parents and grandmother lived at 204 W. Webster St., in Benton.[43]

The Herrin Massacre took place on June 22, 1922, and one account from nine years later included Pulliam. "He is alleged to have been one of the men in a mob of citizens who appeared in the Lester strip mine riot in 1922."[44] While no contemporary accounts have been found that place him in the mob, he did get into trouble that summer less than two weeks later. He, two friends, and one of their women stole a car, six tires worth $400 and an electric fan from the garage of D. M. Parkhill in Benton on the night of July 5. They drove around Benton for a while, lost a couple of men chasing them, then headed to West Frankfort where they stashed the tires and the fan at one of the friends' house. They then took the car back to Benton and abandoned it near the fairgrounds. Authorities arrested the quartet six days later after finding the tires and fan. One of his partners in crime, Willie Marvel of Benton, had worked as a coal miner, at least in 1920, and if still in that line of work, would have been one of the

---

[42] World War I Draft Registration Cards, 1917-1918; Pulliam Inmate File. May 26, 1929. Examination Record; and Art Long. Feb. 4, 1958. "Ex-Hoodlum Comes Out of Hiding." *Nevada State Journal* (Reno, Nev.). 8.

[43] Illinois Statewide Death Index, 1916-1950. Illinois State Archives. Secretary of State website; and 1920 Census of Franklin Co., Illinois. Ancestry.com. Edward was born Sept. 20, 1850, to William and Evelyn Pulliam in Belleville, Ill. He married Marie Clark in St. Clair County on June 18, 1874, and moved to Franklin County in 1877, settling near the area of Buckner. [Carla Pulliam, comp. 1997. *Obits & Tidbits, Franklin County, Illinois, 1915-1919*. Privately published. 98.]

[44] Oct. 7, 1931. "State Puts Max Pulliam Up For Life." *The Daily Independent* (Murphysboro, Ill.). 1.

miners out on strike that summer. Ironically, Marvel's father John had served as deputy sheriff in Franklin County in 1920.[45]

On March 4, 1923, a Franklin County court convicted Pulliam of larceny and sentenced him from one to ten years in the Illinois State Reformatory at Pontiac. At that time minors went to the St. Charles School for Boys and youths in their 20s usually ended up at the Illinois State Reformatory. Only the worst in that age group went directly to a state penitentiary. He earned his parole from there Feb. 2, 1924, in part by working as a trusty and not attempting to escape. He discharged his parole completely on Feb. 3, 1925.[46]

So in world of orphans and father-less youths joining the criminal gangs of Prohibition, how did Pulliam with his well-established family get involved? "How does any ornery young punk get mixed up in something like that?" he reflected as an old man, "I didn't go into those things blind. My eyes were wide open. I got old too early, smart too late."[47]

The murder of Caesar Cagle and the attack on the Herrin Hospital by the Ku Klux Klan took place a week after his release, but neither newspaper reports, nor Johnson's own testimony show him to be involved. Only Jack Skelcher of the known Shelton gangsters did Johnson specifically mention as being present that night in addition to Carl and Earl Shelton.

Johnson claimed he took part in the first shootout at the Smith

---

[45] July 13, 1922. "Arrest Four For Robbing Local Garage." *Benton Republican* (Benton, Ill.). 1; and 1920 Census of Franklin Co., Illinois. Ancestry.com. Years later on June 28, 1933, Marvel pled guilty to armed robbery in Franklin County Circuit Court. He received a sentence of one year to life at the Southern Illinois Penitentiary, now Menard Correctional Center. [Carla Pulliam, comp. 2002. *The Daily American, West Frankfort, Illinois, 1933*. Privately published. 98.]

[46] Illinois State Reformatory. Pontiac Master Index 1985-1927. Illinois State Archives, Springfield, Ill.; and Max Pulliam Inmate File.

[47] Art Long. Feb. 4, 1958. "Ex-Hoodlum Comes Out of Hiding in Nevada." *Nevada State Journal* (Reno, Nev.). 8.

Garage in Herrin in August 1924. If he did, and it's not clear since his story differs greatly from other accounts, and if Pulliam is Johnson, then Pulliam must have joined the Shelton Gang almost immediately after his parole. One witness to the event did testify at the coroner's inquest that some 40 men took part in the shooting, which was far greater number than the sheriff's version or even most of the Klan sympathizers.

Three months after the shootout in front of Smith's Garage, another mass gunfight almost broke out in the streets of East St. Louis outside the federal courthouse on a day when the court heard a number of Herrin liquor cases. The clash took place at high noon on Nov. 19, after closing arguments in the case of Nicholas Trasbaski. While the jury deliberated the Klan witnesses exited the building and saw a Dodge touring car containing Ralph Johnson, R. A. Livingston, Bernard Shelton and Charles Brown. Three of the men stepped out and started a shouting match with the Herrin Klansmen. If deputy U.S. marshals and the East St. Louis police hadn't intervened a bloodbath might have easily ensued. Police arrested the four anti-Klansman along with one of the Klan witnesses for carrying concealed weapons. They released the anti-Klansmen after they filed $500 bonds. So far this is the only record of "Johnson" outside the articles found so far. Charlie Briggs used Brown as one of his aliases. Livingston may have been another alias as well. Like Johnson, this is about the only time it surfaces in the papers along with one of the Shelton brothers. Other gangsters "noted in the streets" that day but not arrested included Carl Shelton and Art Newman.[48]

---

[48] Oldham Paisley (5 & 6) 49-50. Two articles from the next day on Nov. 20, 1924, tell the story. "Made Arrests in Fear of a Riot," most likely ran in the *Marion Evening Post* which copied much the story from the *St. Louis Globe-Democrat*, and "Many Are Fined at East St. Louis" from the *Marion Daily Republican*.

Johnson never wrote that he took part in the Election Day riot at Herrin in April 1926, but from all appearances he told it as an eyewitness, particularly with the behind-the-scene details such as "Blackie" Armes' sweet smell that day.

After the riot the governor sent the National Guard into Herrin to maintain order. In general that worked, the presence of the soldiers kept the gangs and the Klan from another wholesale gun battle. It didn't prevent small level assaults and one-on-one murders. On the morning of June 25, three Herrin residents discovered the body of an unknown man on the "Weaver road north of Herrin near the Iron Mountain railroad." He wore "a complete suit of denim overalls over a pair of light trousers and white shirt," and had been shot in the jaw. He carried a .38 caliber revolver and ammunition which had been left on him. The only clue to his identity came from a cap with a tag from a St. Louis clothing store. Years later Birger gangster Harvey Dungey identified him as "Pretty Boy," a St. Louis gangster brought down to Herrin to help the Shelton Gang. Instead of helping, Birger had Steve George use him for target practice with a machine gun.[49]

Throughout June and early July a series of fights and assaults that took place that on the surface appeared to be between the gangs and Klan members, since the attackers generally represented known enemies of the Klan. The victims included Albert Blue, Paul Benton, a night waiter at the Jefferson Hotel and Ray Hancock who had been clubbed over the head while sitting in his car. However, when reporters asked, Klan leaders denied the victims had been members. Finally on July 7, Herrin Mayor

---

[49] Paisley 5 & 6. June 25, 1926. "Armed Stranger Found Slain Near Herrin." *Marion Daily Republican* (Marion, Ill.); and Harvey Dungey. [n.d.] Drawing #20. Harvey Dungey Collection. Franklin County Jail Museum.

Marshall McCormack declared war on the gangsters ordering police to "arrest all gangmen in the city and lodge them in jail unless they could show some means of support." Using the state's vagrancy laws, police started by arresting "Blackie" Armes and Ray Walker that morning. Any other gangsters found also made the list. In addition, the state's attorney filed charges against Armes, Bernie and Earl Shelton as well as Ray and Harry Walker for assault with a deadly weapon in the attack on Benton the day before.[50]

On the surface it all made sense. The mayor had legitimate grounds to go after the gangsters. As a former Klan leader who had left the Klan to run for mayor the move could be seen to secure additional political support. In fact, as testimony would later show, McCormack, his police chief, his brother who was also a policeman and the state's attorney had all joined in cahoots with Charlie Birger. All four eventually would serve time in the federal penitentiary at Leavenworth. The vagrancy charges against the gangsters didn't stick though. The city judge, himself aligned with the Sheltons, dismissed the case due to lack of evidence.[51]

The cleanup campaign had the additional effect of targeting the Shelton Brothers' allies in the city, including Pulliam. The Sheltons for the most part had returned to East St. Louis, but the Armes and Walker brothers continued to serve as the gang's muscle in Herrin. Pulliam's role, at least according to the *Marion Evening Post* which maintained close ties with the Shelton Gang,

---

[50] Paisley 5 & 6. July 7, 1926. "Herrin Mayor In Campaign to Rid City of Gunmen." *Marion Daily Republican* (Marion, Ill.).

[51] Paul M. Angle. 1952. *Bloody Williamson: A Chapter in American Lawlessness*. 1952. New York: Alfred A. Knopf. 236; Feb. 23, 1929. "Ex-Mayor of Herrin Gets Two Year Sentence." *Jefferson City Post-Tribune* (Jefferson City, Mo.). 1; and Aug. 27, 1926. "Raid Herrin Hotel Arsenal." *The Free Press* (Carbondale, Ill.). 1.

called Pulliam "the brain" of the Herrin band, "the others follow out his orders explicitly."[52]

Johnson dated the split between the Birger and Carl Shelton to early July so the mayor's clean-up campaign offered too perfect a timing.

On July 12, Harry Walker killed "Oklahoma Curley." On Aug. 16, Johnson's successor as collector for the slot machines, John Howard, died in Saline county after being shot outside a Harco pool hall. Six days later unknown gunmen killed Harry Walker and Everett Smith at a roadhouse north of Marion.[53]

Five days later on Aug. 27, Mayor McCormack, his entire police force and two National Guard officers peaceably raided the Palace Hotel on North Park Avenue and arrested Pulliam, "Blackie" Armes and two other youths later released. The four offered no resistance. There in the hotel rooms, Pulliam and the others possessed a small armory of weapons confiscated by the police. The guns included "a number of sawed off shot guns, a quantity of rifles, and 25 or 30 revolvers of various makes."[54]

Benld Bank Robbery

When Pulliam and his fellow Sheltonites didn't pick fights in Herrin they looked around to make some easy money elsewhere. On July 29, six members of the gang attempted to rob the Benld State Bank in Macoupin Co., Illinois.

As the Associated Press put it, "Plans to rob the Benld State bank were frustrated late last night when Benld police arrested two bandits, fought a running gun battle with four others,

---

[52] Paisley (5 & 6) 35. Sept. 15, 1926. "Mack Pulliam, In An..." *Marion Evening Post* (Marion, Ill.). 1.

[53] Gary DeNeal lii-liii.

[54] Paisley (5 & 6) 34. "Herrin Mayor in Active Drive on Armed Gangmen."

capturing one and forcing the [other] three to desert their auto. The entire population was aroused by the noise of the battle which place in the city park."

Held in the county jail at Carlinville, the three would-be bank robbers gave up aliases of Esau Burchfield; Isadore Kapz and Max Schlarr, all from either Decatur, Illinois, or Michigan. In reality Pulliam and the two Armes brothers provided the aliases. Carl Shelton arrived later that day along with his brother Bernie and posted $9,000 cash for their bonds. "On that occasion Carl Shelton is said to have flashed a badge indicating he was a deputy sheriff of Williamson county."

The gangsters didn't know at the time someone had tipped off the bank that they were about to be held up. The identity of that tipster has never been discovered, which might explain the gang's response a few weeks later. When Pulliam and some of the others involved in the Benld job found an investigator from the Burns Detective Agency in the lobby of the Palace Hotel they immediately assumed he worked on behalf of the bank. They kidnapped him and forced him upstairs where they tortured him. The detective hadn't realized the danger. He had simply been assigned to recover a car for a creditor.

"The detective reported he was sitting in the lobby of the Palace hotel one morning when he was seized from behind and covered by seven armed men, who took him upstairs to a room. Here the armed men accused the detective of being a Burns man assigned to banks. He denied this, and was struck several times. His jaw was fractured in three places, and he lost teeth. The gangsters then sought information from him concerning another Burns detective and resented his silence. The detective said his clothing was stripped from him, and he was burned with lighted cigars and cigarettes. Then they took his detective's badge, No 49, from his coat, and pricked him 49 times with the pin of the badge. Finally, after being detained in the room for five hours he was given his clothing and told to 'Get the hell out of here.'"[55]

Targeting Pulliam and Holland

Pulliam's arrests for the bank robbery and the firearms in Herrin didn't spread his name around nearly as much as getting shot and surviving on Sept. 12. Even the *New York Times* ran with it though the wire story misspelled his first name as "Mack."

Historians today generally identify Charlie Birger as the man responsible for most, if not all, of the gangland killings in Bloody Williamson in the latter part of 1926, even though many of the victims belonged to his side. Some knew too much for the authorities and represented too big a liability to let live. Others in the case of Lyle "Shag" Worsham, he believed, reported back to the Sheltons. He feared the presence of such spies in his midst because he likely had at least one inside the Shelton Gang. Someone tipped off the Benld State Bank in July, and some accounts of the Sept. 12 hit on Pulliam and Holland suggested Carl Shelton as the actual target, and the attack took place at that location because Birger thought Shelton would be present.

Around 1 or 1:30 a.m. Sunday morning, Sept. 12, unknown gunmen fired on Pulliam's auto, an ivory-colored sport model Oakland roadster with a blue strip around the body, where he, his

---

[55] July 29, 1926. "Police of Benld Fight With Band of Bank Robbers." *Freeport Journal-Standard* (Freeport, Ill.). 11; and Nov. 11, 1926. "Gunmen Torture Burns Detective at Herrin Hotel." *The Free Press* (Carbondale, Ill.). Ward "Casey" Jones told this story to a reporter for the *St. Louis Star*, but dated it to Sept. 18, 1926. That's not likely correct if Pulliam took part. He had been shot just six days earlier and would still have been recuperating.

wife and William "Wild Bill" Holland, all sat in the front seat.[56]

"According to information given out following the shooting, Holland [and] the Pulliams were in a car passing a two story house on the Herrin road, when they were fired upon from ambush. The Pulliams said they had been to a dance and were returning him at the time attacked. They refused to ascribe any cause for the attack, although they are said to be friends of Everett Smith and Harry Walker who were killed recently near Marion, which is believed by some to have a bearing upon the case."

Johnson didn't provide much information about Holland, just one of the mentioned who "held forth" at Bernie Shelton's joint on the north side of Herrin. Born June 23, 1905, in Herrin, Holland was 21 years, two months and 19 days old at the time of his death. He worked as a coal miner at Consolidated Coal Company's No. 7 mine and still lived with his mother at 321 N. 12th St., the eldest of at least six children. "Holland had lived at Herrin for many years with his mother, who had been told by her son of threats upon his life. He had warned her if he ever met a certain fellow, someone would be killed, but he did not tell her who the party was."[57] He had been the leading bread winner for the family since his father's death on April 30, 1923. The family wasn't perfect by any means. His father had killed a man, Ezra Cox, at Weaver, two years earlier.[58]

As for Holland the writer at the *Marion Evening Post* with the close Shelton Gang ties noted, "the dead man [is] said to have

---

[56] There wouldn't have been a backseat in Pulliam's roadster.

[57] Sept. 13, 1926. "William Holland Shot to Death." *Herrin Daily Journal* (Herrin, Ill.). 1; 1920 Census of Williamson Co., Illinois. Ancestry.com; and Paisley (5 & 6) 36; "Wm. H. Holland." *Marion Evening Post* (Marion, Ill.).

[58] Illinois Statewide Death Index; Aug. 23, 1921. "Miner is Fatally Stabbed at Herrin." *Mt. Vernon Register-News* (Mt. Vernon, Ill.). 1.

been one of the rum runners for one of the two leading organizations in this county." The next summer a wrap-up of the gang war described Holland as "said to have been a body guard of the Sheltons..." At the height of the gang war in November 1926, Earl Shelton described him as a "young miner... a dear little mild-mannered chap, 18 years old, who wouldn't have offended anyone. He was so mild that we called him 'Wild Bill.'" Shelton also blamed Birger as the killer.[59]

While contemporary accounts don't mention Carl Shelton as a target, one of Birger's gangsters described what he heard about the incident in a letter he wrote decades later. Shelton may have been the target himself, but Birger had to settle for killing Holland. "It happened during a raid by the Birger gang on a roadhouse between Johnston City and Herrin. The Sheltons were known to be there at the time of the raid, and those that could, got away, fled — except for "Wild Bill" and Pat Pulliam and his wife — also shot in the gun battle."[60] Again, someone seemed to tip off Birger that night to the Sheltons whereabouts. Luckily for Carl, someone may have tipped him off as well that Birger was on his way. Five days later Birger may have found out that Worsham had been the snitch in his gang as he ordered him killed on the 17th.

The contemporary accounts don't give a clear picture of what took place on the morning of the 12th, and the second-hand story

---

[59] Paisley (5 & 6) 36, 92. "Wm. H. Holland." *Marion Evening Post* (Marion, Ill.) and "Shelton Boys Say They're Out of Williamson County For Good"; and Oldham Paisley, comp. 2006. *Newspaper Articles from Oldham Paisley's Scrapbooks: Vol. 7 & 8, Birger & Trial.* Marion, Ill.: Williamson County Historical Society, 15; "Southern Illinois Gangster Warfare Passing in Review."

[60] DeNeal 119. DeNeal didn't identify the gangster, but he talked to at least two members of the gang for his book, and possibly more. He identified Riley "Alabam" Simmons as well as one other member not identified in his writings as taking a part in the kidnapping of Lory and Ethel Price.

from the elderly Birger gangster doesn't clarify matters. None of the news stories mention any other members of the Shelton Gang, only Holland, Pulliam and his wife. The Associated Press placed the attack on the concrete road three miles east of Herrin. One local account stated they were "passing a two story house on the Herrin road" when the ambush took place, implying the ambush came as they drove by. Another account based on Pulliam's testimony at the inquest placed it near the C.B.&Q Railroad (now the Burlington-Northern Railroad) which crosses Stotlar Road about a half mile east of the Herrin City Cemetery. There, the men went inside a two-story building near the tracks. Johnson called it "Gene's Place," other accounts imply the name as "Grover's Place." Regardless of the name when they came out two men advanced toward them as they got into Pulliam's car.[61]

"According to Pulliam, the guns included a machine gun, and from the looks of the Oakland roaster, two or three machine guns were used. It was literally punctured with bullets, from buck shot to large caliber revolver. More than eighteen shots entered the body of Holland, whose right thumb was shot off, left leg broken in several places, with fatal wounds about the chest, head and arteries."

As for Pulliam, bullets struck him in the right arm and back. One bullet entered in the ribs and the other breaking his collar bone. For a time, doctors wondered if they would be able to save his arm after the bullet shattered the bone. Pulliam's wife received two wounds as well, one bullet "shot through the fleshy part of the right thigh" as well as "several buckshot lodged in her right

---

[61] Part of the discrepancy over the name may be due to multiple roadhouses in the area. Three joints stood side by side where Smith and Walker lost their lives a month earlier. Likewise Birger had interest in two joints across the road from each other at Halfway in 1923.

arm." The Pulliams survived the shooting only because Max "kicked the door open" so he and Mildred could roll "out of the car upon the ground where they remained until the shooting stopped." The following year Rado Millich, one of Birger's gangsters testified that the Pulliams only survived that night because Ward "Casey" Jones' machine gun had jammed.[62]

Someone from Grover's Place took Pulliam and his wife to Herrin Hospital. Another unknown person drove the Oakland and parked it in front of the hospital where it sat 45 minutes to an hour before someone found Holland's dead body sitting inside.[63]

They called police and night officer George Wright had the unpleasant task of investigating the body. Years later Wright told what he saw: "He was sitting there, his eyeballs were out on his cheeks. He'd been shot in the back of his head — I suppose with a shotgun with slugs. I walked around on that side and opened the door — back in those days cars had running boards — and a thumb fell out on the running board. It was off of him."

But even with all that, he had not suffered his last indignity. Pulliam told Wright that Holland had $50 in his pockets. "George, go down there and go through Bill's pockets... his old mother will need that." Wright told the undertaker who looked but they only found a dime. "Somebody had rolled him after they shot him."[64]

Up until the attack, Pulliam had his parents fooled as to his real occupation. His father told the press he thought his son worked as a traveling salesman, which he did in a way. The

---

[62] C. Bishop Hill. [n.d., but likely 1927]. *Complete History of Southern Illinois' Gang War.* Privately published. 43. The Williamson County Historical Society has republished the book.

[63] Sept. 13, 1926. "William Holland Shot to Death." *Herrin Daily Journal* (Herrin, Ill.). 1; and Paisley (5 & 6) 36. "Wm. H. Holland." *Marion Evening Post* (Marion, Ill.); and "Make Another Attack on Life of M. Pulliam." *Marion Daily Republican* (Marion, Ill.).

[64] DeNeal 118-119.

younger Pulliam's merchandise consisted more in the line of alcohol, slot machines and prostitutes rather than the flour, feed, sugar, salt, milk, malt syrup and canned goods listed on the elder Pulliam's letterhead.

At the time of the shooting the most of the press considered Holland the target. That changed however two days later when the Birger and his men viciously targeted Pulliam himself.

Shortly after Max and his wife arrived at the hospital Sunday morning operators transferred a mysterious call to the hospital administration. "The party inquiring wanted to know who was injured, dead, etc., and when told it was Holland, Pulliam and Pulliam's wife, is alleged to have concluded with 'That's good.'" At first, Pulliam's injuries prevented transport to another facility, but by Tuesday his condition had stabilized enough to do so. Pulliam's parents had no illusions their son's attackers would recognize the hospital's hallways inviolate. Residents could still point to the bullet holes on the front facade from the Klan's fusillade two years earlier. Just five months earlier Dr. Black himself had to exit over the roof to escape the Klan after the Election Day riot across the street in April. The Pulliams knew they needed to move Max to a safer location. Afraid the hospital had eyes and ears more loyal to Birger than the Sheltons, they arranged for Benton undertaker Ed Nolen and his son Joe to pick Max up in their ambulance.

"How the opposing side learned of Pulliam's transfer will probably never be told," the *Marion Evening Post* reported. "None of the ambulance drivers at Herrin had any knowledge of who drove the injured toward Benton... No doubt a spotter has been on the job since the injured were taken to Herrin, with an intent of keeping a trace of Pulliam, who is believed to know more than he has told about the shooting Sunday a.m."

About 2:30 p.m. Nolen's combination coach, an ambulance for the living and a hearse for the dead, left Herrin Hospital in what organizers hoped would look like a funeral procession for the 20-mile trip to the Benton hospital. If Nolen drove slow the trip could have easily taken a hour to go through Johnston City and West Frankfort. Nolen and his son rode in front while Max Pulliam stretched out on a cot in the back where the undertakers would normally have carried a casket. Inside, toward the back near his head his mother Nora sat probably tenderly stroking his cheeks, offering words of encouragement and all the tiny things mothers do when sickness strikes their loved ones. One of Pulliam's friends, "Strawberry" Wells, sat near his feet looking out the back window. In the three cars that followed, Ed Russell drove the first, Max's father Fred Pulliam the second, and Pulliam's wife rode with her father, Bert Stewart, in the third.

At Johnston City, Fred realized he forgot the x-rays and returned to Herrin. North of West Frankfort Birger's driver pulled up alongside Russell's car. A gangster yelled out the window asking who was in the ambulance. Russell answered and the gangsters strongly suggested he turn around. Behind him, Stewart realized the danger and immediately took off in another direction. Sure in their knowledge of Pulliam's location, Birger's car sped up to catch the ambulance. Inside Wells looked out the back window and saw Birger's car. "We're in for it," he exclaimed.

Birger's vehicle drew up even with the ambulance and ordered Nolen to pull over. Instead, he picked up his speed trying to close a two or three mile gap between him and the Benton square. Birger ordered his driver to pass and block the road. With nowhere to go and five or six men with guns in front of him,

Nolen pulled to a stop about a mile outside Benton near the Masonic and Odd Fellows Cemetery. Birger ordered the Nolens and Wells out of the ambulance.

As his men held weapons on them, Birger and another gangster, one with a machine gun and the other a shotgun, but both with revolvers, entered the back of the ambulance. Birger ordered Mrs. Pulliam out, but she refused, even with a machine gun rammed into her side. Birger and his man climbed in and started beating Pulliam's head with the butts of their revolvers. "[We] conked that fellow until he fainted away," Birger described a month later. By the third attack, Mrs. Pulliam placed her own body in the way and took the blow on her arm. Frustrated Birger told Pulliam he was lucky, "Well, we don't intend to kill a woman to get you." He then got out, gathered his men and left, leaving Pulliam bleeding and unconscious.[65]

One of the undated stories about Pulliam that probably took place in the fall of 1926 during the height of the Gang War shows a link to Johnson's account of the dynamite bombs favored by the Shelton Gang. During his research on Charlie Birger some three decades ago, Gary DeNeal talked to one of Birger's bartenders who had his own joint blown up, which he blamed on Pulliam himself. His joint was apparently closed at the time and it was either just him there sleeping, or him and another woman. "Following the excitement," DeNeal wrote the man, "walked down the highway as 'naked as a jaybird.'" Even in the half

---

[65] Sept. 15, 1926. "Pulliam Beaten by Six Gangsters." *Herrin Daily Journal* (Herrin, Ill.). 1; Sept. 15, 1926. "Armed Men Attack Pulliam In Ambulance On Way to Hospital." *The Daily Independent* (Murphysboro, Ill.). 1; Sept. 15, 1926. "Wounded Herrin Man Beat Up in Ambulance." *The Free Press*. (Carbondale, Ill.). 2; Paisley (5 & 6) 35-37. Sept. 15, 1926. "Make Another Attack on Life of Pulliam" *Marion Daily Republican* (Marion, Ill.), and Sept. 15, 1926. "Mack Pulliam, in an...." *Marion Evening Post* (Marion, Ill.); Carla Pulliam, comp. 1998. *The Daily American, West Frankfort, Illinois, 1925-1926*. Privately published. 103; and DeNeal 120.

century that had passed by, the bartender "still remembered the name of the woman who saw him on the road."[66]

Overall, he spent his time during the Klan War and the Gang War, "in trouble in Williamson and Franklin County on numerous occasions," the U.S. Attorney later noted.[67]

After Secrets

Around the last part of January 1927, while millions across the country read the serial installments of "Secrets of the Herrin Gangs" as told by Ralph Johnson, Pulliam and his wife moved to Springfield where they rented an apartment. Although Johnson told of going into hiding, Joe McGlynn, the ever-present Shelton attorney, managed to stay in contact. At the end of the month Pulliam's wife agreed to testify on behalf of Carl, Earl and Bernie in the upcoming Collinsville mail robbery trial. In reality she agreed to commit perjury on the stand in order to help the brothers go free. If any friction existed between Pulliam and the Sheltons over Johnson's accounts, her actions might have represented the price to be paid to ease back into their good graces.

On Feb. 4th, Mildred testified in federal court at Quincy, Illinois, that Birger and Newman actually told her and Max that they were going to "get the Sheltons on that Collinsville job." Both men, along with Birger gangster Harvey Dungey lied on the stand

---

[66] DeNeal xlii. DeNeal didn't name the bartender and keeps his promise of anonymity to his sources decades later even long after their deaths – an admirable trait that speaks well of his character, even if it is mildly irritating to other researchers. It's possible that Pulliam was attempting to avenge his own shooting by attacking someone who took part in the shooting, or the subsequent ambulance attack. It's probably not the attack on Shaw's Garden that Johnson wrote about. Roy Shaw died in 1962. [Nov. 29, 1962. "Former Area Man Dies." *Southern Illinoisan* (Carbondale, Ill.). 11.]

[67] Max Pulliam Inmate File. "Parole Report By United States Attorney."

repeatedly in an effort to secure a long trip to Leavenworth for the Sheltons. Mildred just lied to help the Sheltons. While it certainly fit Birger's personality to brag about something like getting the Sheltons, it's hard to imagine the Pulliams still going to Shady Rest in September 1926, with the gang war breaking out into the open. She claimed the visit took place just a few days before they survived the ambush that killed Holland.

She also named Birger and Newman as the two men who ambushed them. While others named Birger as one of the shooters, Newman had previously told reporters he still resided in Miami, Florida, until later that month.

When asked about her husband's whereabouts, she said she didn't know. He might be in New Orleans, she thought.[68] In the end her testimony didn't help enough. The jury found the Sheltons guilty and judge sentenced them to 25 years at Leavenworth.[69]

On March 11, Springfield police arrested Pulliam and his wife at a local rooming house where they had resided for about six weeks as suspects "responsible for several crimes in the region of Springfield over a period of a month." Neither would admit to any crimes in the city and police found no evidence apparently. However they did find a reason to hold the pair when they discovered narcotics in their room. While in police custody, postal inspectors questioned him about the robbery of the Woodlawn post office two years earlier in Jefferson Co., Illinois. Apparently they were satisfied by his answers, the police released him. Meanwhile, a federal grand jury at Quincy indicted both Pulliams

---

[68] Paisley 9:112-113; Feb. 3, 1927. "Shelton Defense Rests Case and Attorneys Begin Arguments To Jury - Shelton Story Rebutted." *Marion Daily Republican* (Marion, Ill.).

[69] Feb. 6, 1927. "Convicted of Mail Robbery." *The Abilene Morning Reporter-News* (Abilene, Texas). 1.

for violating the federal anti-narcotics Harrison Act. Eventually though the U.S. Attorney dismissed the case.[70]

By this time Pulliam had become addicted to dope as pain relief for the gunshot wounds and subsequent beating that Birger gave him. His body still carried two of the bullets. He and his wife continued their crime spree cumulating with a robbery at Edwards and Shapman dry cleaners in Springfield on Saturday, April 23. There Pulliam and a possible partner, Pete Hungate of Benton, wore masks as they held guns on the employees, as Mildred Pulliam, unmasked, but dressed in men's clothing and short haircut, reached into the cash register and "scooped up $400 in currency."

For some reason still unexplained, 15 minutes after leaving the dry cleaners, and likely just after the dry cleaners' employees had called the police, Mildred made her own call to the authorities. She called the Sangamon County Jail, identified herself, then asked permission to see two female prisoners. The clerk told her no visitors were allowed after 5 p.m. Later he noted that Mildred "talked excitedly" and "refused to say where she had made the call." Somehow police officials were able to determine where she had made the call and ordered officers to trail her. Police arrested her the next day as the "bob-haired bandit" wanted for the robbery.

With his wife arrested Pulliam and Hungate high-tailed it out of the capital and back toward home. That Sunday evening

---

[70] March 12, 1927. "Grill Member of Shelton Gang." *Decatur Evening Herald* (Decatur, Ill.). 1; March 12, 1927. "Pulliam Questioned by Springfield Police." *The Daily Independent* (Murphysboro, Ill.). 1; and March 22, 1927. "2 Members of Shelton Gang Are Indicted." *Alton Evening Telegraph* (Alton, Ill.). 2; also Max Pulliam Inmate File. J. E. Hoover. July 12, 1929. Letter to Supt. of Prisons, Dept. of Justice; and Chief of Police, Springfield, Ill. July 22, 1929. Letter to T. B. White, Warden, Leavenworth.

Pulliam wrecked his car at Zeigler, breaking his ribs and adding other injuries as well to his battered body. Authorities easily arrested the pair near Benton shortly thereafter. Luckily for the duo the laundry's employees didn't recognize them. Police released them that Thursday. Likewise when Mildred's preliminary hearing came up on May 3, the same employees who identified her previously found they couldn't in court. With the case in tatters, the court released her.[71]

The same week Pulliam dealt with the robbery fallout, the Sheltons found a way to secure their own freedom out of Leavenworth. They knew Birger, Newman and Dungey had lied on the stand in their mail robbery trial in February, they just needed a way to prove it. That proof came wrapped up in a confession by Dungey, who had since split with Birger.

Dungey by this time had formed his own gang based out of his roadhouse, the Dew Drop Inn, south of West Frankfort. The second night after Birger made bail on the Adams murder charge and returned to Harrisburg, Dungey and three other men attempted to burn down Birger's home with the gang leader still in it on the morning of March 22. Birger heard them and grabbed a machine gun. He started shooting and managed to hit Dungey once, wounding him. All of the men got away though. Dungey also claimed that Birger had Connie Ritter and Ernest Blue try to ambush him in March though it's not clear which incident took place first.[72]

---

[71] April 26, 1927. "Shelton Gang Woman, Bobbed Hair Bandit." *The Free Press* (Carbondale, Ill). 3; April 26, 1927. "Mrs. Max Pulliam Held As Robber Accomplice." *The Daily Independent* (Murphysboro, Ill). 2; April 27, 1927. "Max Pulliam Arrested." *The Daily Independent* (Murphysboro, Ill). 2; and May 3, 1927. "Mrs. Pulliam Released." *The Daily Independent* (Murphysboro, Ill). 1.

[72] March 22, 1927. "Birger Routs Intruders Who Try to Fire Home." *Logansport Pharos-Tribune* (Logansport, Ind). 6; and Harvey Dungey. Drawings #85, #87 and captions.

On Wednesday, April 28, Dungey signed an affidavit declaring he had not seen the Sheltons in Collinsville the morning of the mail robbery and had committed perjury on the witness stand due to death threats from Birger and Newman. On Thursday, Birger received a double blow. That morning, while still sleeping the Franklin County Sheriff arrived with his deputies to arrest him on new charges involving Joe Adams' murder. Hours later in Springfield, the Sheltons' attorney filed Dungey's affidavit and a motion for a new trial. While Birger headed back to jail his enemies would soon go free. [73]

Birger may have got even with Dungey. On May 2, someone burned down the Dew Drop Inn. Birger tried to undercut Dungey's testimony telling the press that the Sheltons had bought the affidavit, having offered $10,000 to anyone who could help get their convictions overturned.[74] Meanwhile, the Shelton Brothers made their plans to return to Illinois. A few weeks later they arrived in the state free men.

As part of their plans for returning Carl Shelton reached out to Pulliam. On April 26, the same Monday that Pulliam found himself arrested for the dry cleaners robbery, and two days before Dungey's formal affidavit, Carl wrote to Pulliam from his cell in Leavenworth. He addressed his letter to Pulliam's alias, Pat Pulliam and sent it in care of a friend, Bob Summers at 205 ½ N. 6th St. in Springfield.[75]

After his near scrapes in Springfield, Pulliam got back into the

[73] April 28, 1927. "Sheltons To Ask Re-Trial." *Decatur Evening Herald* (Decatur, Ill.). 1; April 28, 1927. "Says He Lied on Sheltons, New Trial Is Asked." *Carbondale Free Press* (Carbondale, Ill.). 1.

[74] May 3, 1927. "Property of Birger Foe is Destroyed." *Decatur Review.* (Decatur, Ill.); and April 29, 1927. "Charlie Birger, Gangster, Held in Murder Case." *Sterling Daily Gazette* (Sterling, Ill.). 1.

[75] Carl Shelton (#27024) Inmate File. Leavenworth Inmate Files. National Archives-Kansas City. J. E. Hoover. Mar. 1, 1927. Letter to Superintendent of Prisons. The actual address is now part of the Abraham Lincoln Presidential Library.

liquor distribution business, possibly even back with the Sheltons once they were arrived back from Leavenworth. On Sept. 16, the law caught up to Pulliam again, this time in the Chicago suburb of Wheaton, Illinois, and arrested him as a "Beer-Runner." He apparently got out of that fix, possibly by the simple ruse of paying for his bond and then leaving town.[76]

He still spent time in Benton though. On Aug. 7, 1928, police sought him out for arrest after two other men had been shot and wounded during a possible hold-up at Earl Kreiger's joint near West Frankfort.

"Information concerning the affair has been very meager. Officers said they were informed that Kreiger and [Teddy] Newrock were in the house, which is a short distance west of the hard road just south of the city limits, when three men came up in an automobile and, entering the house, ordered them to 'put 'em high.' During the gun play which followed Newrock and [Bill] Trout were wounded."[77]

Troutt, the story implied, took part in the hold-up, though he claimed, "that he walked into the place and that 'the first thing he knew he was shot.'" His story might be believable if he didn't have a future history with Pulliam conducting armed robberies. Kreiger or somebody had the sense to write down the robber's license plate. From that number or just Newrock's own memory, police soon learned that need to find Pulliam. Other than identifying Pulliam as a suspect, the newspaper never covered any updates in the robbery. Troutt, who friends thought might die from the gunshot to his shoulder, recovered only to be shot again

---

[76] Max Pulliam Inmate File.

[77] Although newspaper regularly spelled Troutt's name as Trout, his death certificate and tombstone both use the Troutt spelling.

two years later in another holdup with Pulliam.[78]

The other man, "Teddy Newrock," a roadhouse operator allied with Charlie Birger, would have known Pulliam from those days as well. Born in 1894, Newrock immigrated to America from Poland in 1907, and became a naturalized citizen in 1914. He settled at West Frankfort where he operated a service car in 1917. By 1920, like most men there he worked as a coal miner. Eventually he turned to bootlegging and crime.[79]

Besides operating a roadhouse, Newrock stayed close enough to Birger for Clarence Rone to identify him as one of the men present when Dungey and two others killed Lyle "Shag" Worsham on Sept. 17, 1926, three days after Birger and the gang attacked Pulliam in the ambulance. Newrock also rode with Dungey and Birger on the day of Joe Adams assassination on Dec. 10, 1926. That night Birger assigned Newrock the job of keeping tabs on the eldest of the two brothers hired for the job. Newrock and Harry Thomasson checked into Harrisburg's Horning Hotel as "John Winters" and "James Madison."[80]

Although indicted in 1927 for his part in the Worsham killing Newrock managed to avoid capture until Dec. 2, 1927, three days before the start of the trial. At the time of his arrest in Carbondale, he carried coded telegrams "believed to be horse race tips" as well

---

[78] Aug. 8, 1928. "2 Shot During Alleged Holdup, Kreiger Place." *The Daily American* (West Frankfort, Ill.). 1; and Aug. 8, 1928. "Benton Man Shot Tuesday at Frankfort." *Benton Evening News* (Benton, Ill.). 1.

[79] Social Security Death Index. Rootsweb.com; World War I Draft Registration Cards, 1917-1918; and 1920 Census of Franklin Co., Illinois. Nawrocki appears to be his legal name as it's the one he used in his draft registrations for both world wars. Illinois issued his Social Security card under the name Newrock, which is also the spelling in his obituary. DeNeal spelled the name Teddy Nurocke. Other spellings included Ted Nierachery, Ted Neurock, and Teddy Newrocky before settling on the simple-to-spell Ted Newrock. In the 1928 stories, the West Frankfort paper identified him as Newrock and the Benton paper, Newrocky.

[80] World War I Draft Registration Cards, 1917-1918; and 1920 Census of Franklin Co., Illinois.

as a number of Chicago and New Orleans names and addresses. He claimed to be bound for New Orleans.[81]

Because of the timing, the state's attorney separated him from the trial so he could move forward against the other defendants. After the jury acquitted the main defendants, including Dungey, the state dropped charges against Newrock. It's also possible that Pulliam and Newrock both planned the robbery. If so, it wouldn't be the first time, or last, that members of the two old gangs got together for a new crime.

By the time Pulliam had his next run in with the law, this time with the feds, prosecutors had mixed feelings about him. The U.S. Attorney noted that the character of Pulliam's associates as well as his habits to industry as "bad," but when asked their opinion as to Pulliam's criminal tendencies, "Do you regard him as a menace to society, an habitual criminal, or as a man who has made a mistake?" the answer came back as "difficult to describe — not of gangster type" but yet an "associate and close friend" of at least certain gangsters. "His connections with the Shelton brothers, bank robbers, mail robbers and liquor runners, were very close."[82]

By the spring of 1929, Pulliam's addiction to pain-killers began to dominate his life. On May 24, he pled guilty in federal court at East St. Louis to nine counts of writing forged prescriptions for narcotics and passing them off to druggists. At the time he faced similar charges at Springfield. He managed to obtain "large quantities in that manner." Judge Wham found it evident that Pulliam obtained the "narcotics to sell," a notion only fortified when Pulliam denied his personal addiction.[83]

---

[81] Dec. 2, 1927. "Nab Gangster Here Wanted on Murder Charge." *The Free Press* (Carbondale, Ill.). 1; Sat., Dec. 3, 1927."Birger Gangsters Ready For Trial." *Decatur Review* (Decatur, Ill.). 5

[82] Max Pulliam Inmate File. Parole Report By United States Attorney.

[83] Paisley 9. May 29, 1929. "Given Two Years on Drug Charges."

A year later his father claimed the conviction came on "meager evidence... produced by an old Doctor that for a number of years has been specializing in Abortion cases and Narcotics. He has killed a lot of people for which he has never been convicted." The elder Pulliam argued that when the government agents "checked upon him, in order to protect himself claimed that his prescription was either forged or raised." Max's father was probably correct in his description, the doctor sounds a lot like someone a dope-addicted gangster familiar with brothels would know. In the end though, it wasn't so much the doctor's testimony, but Pulliam's concern for his wife. The feds had both of them in their sights. If Max would plead guilty, the feds promised to drop the case against Mildred.[84]

Pulliam arrived at Leavenworth a day after his sentencing on May 25, 1929. He listed Mildred as living with his parents at 204 W. Webster St., in Benton and listed his address as Detroit, Michigan, though it's possible the two were switched. He could read and write and had graduated both common school and high school, but not college as he later claimed. While he told the judge he didn't use opium or morphine he told the truth to the prison officials. He also claimed he didn't chew tobacco, but did smoke, and similar to the Sheltons, or at least Carl, he didn't drink.

While in the pen, he had an operation to remove the bullets still lodged in his body from the ambush in 1926. In order to get treatment for his addiction the warden moved Pulliam to the "Annex," which he had to explain to his mother:

"You evidently misunderstand the idea of transferring men of this type there. Our object in it is to best serve them and take them

---

[84] Max Pulliam Inmate File. Fred C. Pulliam. Jan. 5, 1930. Letter to U.S. Board of Pardons & Parole.

away from the criminal type that they are thrown with here and put them together and thus bring about a better medical observation of them... I am sure it will be for his welfare; and the thing for him to do is to co-operate in looking after his betterment."

On Christmas Eve he sent telegrams to Clifford Dickey of Benton, "Merry Christmas to the Hogans and the Dickeys," as well as to Mildred at 3025 E Grand Blvd., Apt. 212, in Detroit, "Love and Merry Christmas to yourself and all the Stewarts."

With a possibility of parole in January 1930, Pulliam's family recruited former Franklin County legislator and *Benton Evening News* publisher Carl Choisser to volunteer to be his first friend or advisor as necessary. Choisser claimed to have personally known Pulliam all of his life and offered to hire him at $20 a week at the paper. When the parole board turned down his petition, his mother again wrote to the warden. "It will soon be 1 year since he was sent there for a crime <u>he did not commit</u>, and not alone for my sake, nor his sake, but in the name of "Justice" I ask you to reconsider." Like her husband who wrote to the parole board listing the problems with the abortionist doctor testified who against his son, Mrs. Pulliam tried as well, "I know you will do this unless there is some good reason or it maybe the District Atty who has never even tried to get the old Dr. who is the real culprit."[85]

It's not clear when, or even if, Max and Mildred separated. In April 1930, the census showed him working as a laborer in the penitentiary at Fort Leavenworth. It listed Pulliam as divorced, but the census for his parents listed both him and his wife as

---

[85] Max Pulliam Inmate File.

residents of their house in Benton, Illinois, though the enumerator wrote "abs" for absent next to both names. As far as the parents knew the two remained married.[86] The correspondence records in his Leavenworth files show both he and his wife sent multiple letters back and forth each month. She sent 15 letters in December 1930, his last month of incarceration. He responded with 10 of his own. In comparison, his mother wrote him six times and he responded twice.

Besides his wife and mother he also corresponded with Stewart Hogan of Benton, a man five years his senior. Hogan's relationship to Pulliam hasn't been determined. One record at Leavenworth listed him as a brother, but other similar records showed no relationship. The parents listed in his obituary don't match Pulliam's. Hogan operated various businesses in West City later in life, including Hogan's Cozy Tavern where sheriff deputies arrested him at least once as a bookie after a gambler reported him to the authorities when he claimed Hogan didn't pay up. Hogan died in Benton at the age of 75 in 1969.[87]

Hogan's later known gambling connections make Pulliam's fourth jail-house correspondent even more interesting. Pulliam wrote to Neil Kerens Pumphrey on Sept. 11, 1930, three months before his term would be up. Pumphrey responded a week later on the 18th. Pulliam replied on the 23rd. Nothing too blatant would have been included in the letters to get past the censors, but Pumphrey's role in the Kansas City and Memphis underworld had already made the attention of the papers.

---

[86] 1930 Census of Leavenworth Co., Kansas; and 1930 Census of Franklin Co., Illinois.

[87] Max Pulliam Inmate File. Correspondence Records; July 19, 1951. "Tavern for Sale" advertisement. *The Daily Register* (Harrisburg, Ill). 4; May 29, 1951. "West City Man Accused as Bookie." *Mt. Vernon Register-News* (Mt. Vernon, Ill.). 6; and April 7, 1969. "Stewart Hogan 75 Dies in Benton." *Southern Illinoisan* (Carbondale, Ill.). 14.

A year earlier, the young professional gambler had been shot in a five-way shootout in front of the prestigious La Salle Hotel in Kansas City that left a Chicago gunman and a St. Louis gangster dead. At the time he and his partners had been meeting with various underworld officials in Kansas City seeking funds to start a major gambling operation at Linn Creek, Mo., where plans to build Bagnell Dam on the Osage River would create the Lake of the Ozarks. Three thousand workers would be hired for the construction project and Pumphrey's crew knew there would be a demand for the workers' entertainment dollars. Their problem turned out to be Ben Barretti, a Chicago gunman who, according to detectives, "attempted to force himself into the gambling organization. Barretti, said by police to have been a notorious killer, was alleged to have been refused a chance to participate because of his reputation."[88]

Pumphrey's father had graduated from the University of Missouri, ran a real estate business in Memphis, and possessed a net worth of a half million dollars, but claimed at the time of his son's shooting that he had spent too much money and too little time with his wayward son. His maternal grandfather had served as an attorney-general for Arkansas. The younger Pumphrey recovered and returned home to Memphis where at least in the census, claimed to work as a real estate salesman with his father and brother.[89]

Pulliam's letters most likely dealt with illegal gambling and its equipment. A month after their correspondence, police in New

---

[88] June 24, 1929. "Two Men Die in Gangster Quarrel." *Moberly Monitor-Index* (Moberly, Mo.). 8; and June 25, 1929. "Continue Probe Into Killing of K.C. Gamblers." *Jefferson City Post-Tribune* (Jefferson City, Mo.). 1.

[89] June 26, 1929. "Easy Life and Lots of Money Spelled Ruin." *Jefferson City Post-Tribune* (Jefferson City, Mo.). 4; and 1910, 1920, and 1930 Censuses of Shelby Co., Tennessee.

York state arrested Pumphrey and four accomplices in a raid on an elaborate gambling den in Sarasota Springs, N.Y. Most interestingly, some of the equipment had been rigged "with a crooked device for fleecing their victims." Pumphrey and one of the men gave aliases, but police in Hot Springs, Ark., provided their real names. At some point previous to this, Pumphrey had been questioned about a bank robbery in Birmingham, Ala. There's no record of Pulliam ever in Hot Springs, but the Arkansas resort was a favorite of the Sheltons. Pumphrey eventually returned to Arkansas and died there the following year on Oct. 28, 1931, in Garland County.[90]

With 144 days allowed for good time, Pulliam managed to cut nearly six months off his two-year sentence. He walked out of Leavenworth on Dec. 31, 1930, with a prison-issued allowance of $15 in cash and a $26.74 train ticket to Detroit on the Missouri Pacific - Wabash Railroad.[91]

'One of the Most Dangerous Men'

While Pulliam presumably met up with Mildred in Detroit at the start of the new year, he ended up back in Franklin County at least by the summer of 1931, and probably without Mildred as she's never mentioned again in connection with him. There he picked up an old accomplice and another man to take advantage of the deteriorating economy. Two years into the Great Depression, the major banks in the county seats and major trade centers of the region had not failed, but bank runs had already wiped out some of the banks in the smaller communities. As more

---

[90] Aug. 16, 1930. "Gambling Place, Saratoga Springs, Raided by Police." *Olean Evening Times* (Olean, N.Y.). 4; and Arkansas Death Index, 1914-1950. Ancestry.com.

[91] Max Pulliam Inmate File. Dec. 31, 1930. Prisoner's Receipt for Discharge Gratuities.

and more individuals began to hoard their money at home, they became targets of criminals like Pulliam who saw an opportunity for easy money. The Union State Bank at Dowell, in northern Jackson County still operated in the summer of 1931, but rumors likely circulated about its condition. With five months it would be closed and the bank president dead from suicide after the board of directors discovered he had embezzled at least $35,000.[92]

In late August 1931, Pulliam, Bill Troutt of Benton, and a third man began a series of home burglaries in Dowell, including the homes of Stanley Shibivitch and Charles Roseman. On Aug. 27, Pulliam and at least one of his partners broke into the house of Isaac Wagoner, robbed and assaulted him with what the grand jury found to be intent to kill. Ironically, Wagoner, one who believed in keeping his money at home, had been an innocent bystander shot in the eye seven years earlier when three bandits robbed the Dowell bank on Sept. 30, 1924.

Pulliam and his partner used a heavy block of wood to ram open Wagoner's door and grilled Wagoner on "the habits of another Dowell man, and the hiding place of the latter's money."[93]

Pulliam's greed got the better of his judgment. They probably were the ones who robbed the widow Rose Halligan around this time as well. A few days later around midnight on Monday, Aug. 31, Pulliam and Troutt tried to rob her again, starting by ramming the same block of wood through her front door. After the first robbery she had wherewithal to shoot first and ask questions later. Luckily for Pulliam, Troutt entered first and took the shots

---

[92] Jan. 12, 1932. "Dowell Bank Looting Loss About $20,000." *The Daily Independent* (Murphysboro, Ill.). 1; and Feb. 17, 1932. "Dowell State Accounts May Recover Half." *The Daily Independent* (Murphysboro, Ill.). 1.

[93] Sept. 30, 1924. "Bank Bandits Shoot Two." *The Free Press* (Carbondale, Ill.). 1; and Sept. 8, 1931. "Pulliam Held on Complaint Dowell Man." *Benton Evening News* (Benton, Ill.). 1

from the fired .45 revolver.

Pulliam managed to get Troutt to the car and back to Benton where he left him on the steps of hospital operated by Dr. Moore around 1 a.m. Either Pulliam or possibly a third accomplice since he wasn't recognized, told the staff a detailed story about how gunmen had robbed and shot Troutt at the Ashley wye farther north on the way back from Peoria, and had taken $80. The driver didn't know anything else, but had just picked up Troutt alongside the road and brought him to the hospital.

By the next morning, the doctors had Troutt on the operating table attempting to remove the two bullets that had penetrated his stomach and back. Once inside they found his intestines had been perforated in 25 places. There was nothing they could do. About 1 a.m. the next morning, Wednesday, Sept. 2, he died, but not before authorities took Wagoner to the hospital where he positively identified Troutt as one of the men who had robbed him the previous week.

On Thursday, his family made funeral arrangements for the following afternoon at East Benton Baptist Church. Pulliam, though didn't make it. On Friday morning O. H. Pugh, assistant state's attorney for Jackson County arrived with Sheriff W. W. Ozburn and Deputy Joe Jennings with a warrant for Pulliam's arrest. Franklin County Deputies Aaron Wells and Byford Vaughn drove over to Pulliam's family home still at 204 W. Webster St., and took Pulliam into custody. As authorities headed back to Murphysboro with their prisoner, Troutt's family buried him alongside his infant daughter in the Masonic and Odd Fellow's Cemetery south of Benton near where Charlie Birger had beaten Pulliam in the ambulance attack just less than 10 days short of five years before.[94]

The Jackson County Grand Jury indicted Pulliam Sept. 18, on charges of burglary against the homes of Wagoner and Roseman, with bond fixed at $15,000 for each indictment. At the time Fletcher Lewis, the Jackson County state's attorney, described Pulliam as "one of the most dangerous men in this section." Law enforcement and the prosecutor continued to hype Pulliam's past as his trial approached named him "one of the worst gangsters in the coal belt." His trial began Oct. 5, 1931, with the press identifying him as "one of the few surviving active Shelton gangsters." In his closing arguments Lewis asked the jury to "put Max Pulliam away for keeps" and they obliged. On the 7th the judge sentenced him to one year to life in the state penitentiary. [95]

Although Pulliam later admitted his guilt to the crimes that sent him to Joliet and Leavenworth, he denied his responsibility for the Dowell burglaries. He claimed he split with the Sheltons in the early 30s, though whether that was due to his incarceration or a conscious decision to break "with the outfit before he was sentenced," as one paper reported years later, is not clear.[96]

---

[94] Carla Pulliam, comp. 2001. *The Daily American, West Frankfort, Illinois, 1931*. Privately published. 105; Sept. 2, 1931. "Bill Trout Succumbs To Wounds." *Benton Evening News* (Benton, Ill.). 1; Sept. 3, 1931. "Trout Funeral Friday Afternoon." *Benton Evening News* (Benton, Ill.). 1; Sept. 4, 1931. "Max Pulliam Arrested Charged With Burglary." *Benton Evening News* (Benton, Ill.). 1; Sept. 5, 1931. "Bent'n Man Shot, Left on Hospital Steps, Burglar." *The Free Press* (Carbondale, Ill.). 1; Sept. 8, 1931. "Pulliam Held on Complaint Dowell Man." *Benton Evening News* (Benton, Ill.). 1; Illinois Statewide Death Index, 1916-1950; and William Troutt tombstone.

[95] Sept. 19, 1931. "Once Bad Man Of Shelton Gang Is Indicted." *The Free Press* (Carbondale, Ill.). 1; The People V. Spiller, 351 Ill. 65 (1932). *Illinois Supreme Court Reports*; Oct. 2, 1931. "Trial of Pulliam, Coal Belt Gangster Here Next Monday." *The Daily Independent* (Murphysboro, Ill.). 1; Oct. 6, 1931. "Ex-Shelton Gang-Man On Trial at Murphysboro." *The Free Press* (Carbondale, Ill.). 1; Oct. 7, 1931. "Gangster Gets 1 to Life Term By Judge Spiller." The Free Press (Carbondale, Ill.). 1; and Oct. 7, 1931. "State Puts Max Pulliam Up For Life." *The Daily Independent* (Murphysboro, Ill.). 1.

[96] Art Long. Feb. 4, 1958. "Ex-Hoodlum Comes Out of Hiding in Nevada." *Nevada State Journal* (Reno, Nev.). 8; and Feb. 5, 1958. "Pat Pulliam Going Back to Illinois." *Nevada State Journal* (Reno, Nev.). 8.

of Dodge. Years later he claimed to have fled first to Indianapolis where he worked as a "rewrite man" at the *Indianapolis Star* before moving to Chicago "for work with a national feature syndicate." Whether this really happened, or was as fictional as his claimed journalism degree from Northwestern University, hasn't been determined. One intriguing connection, the *Indianapolis Star* had just been purchased by a distant relative (and Vice President Dan Quayle's future grandfather) Eugene C. Pulliam the year before.[101] At Chicago, he discovered he had violated parole, and in his words, "so I just took off." He ended up in Nevada and according to one version of his story, worked as a car salesman and real estate agent while living under an assumed name with his family.

A few days later another reporter claimed Pulliam had repudiated the story of living in Nevada under an assume name. Instead, he mentioned he had traveled to Las Vegas once about 10 years earlier to "play some poker." As to a family, deputies didn't think he had one. "He never wrote letters and made no phone calls while in jail here," the reporter wrote. "All sheriff's deputies are sure of is that Pulliam, 59, is wanted in Illinois. Whatever else he said was apparently a Pulliam invention."[102]

After five days in jail, Illinois officials picked him up and began their trip back to the Menard State Penitentiary on the 8th where he would await a court appearance for violating parole. From there Pulliam's life as the unassuming gangster and convict faded into history. Like his two wives before him, the paper trail ends cold without closure. The last reference to him dates more

---

[101] July 1, 2003. "A History of the Indianapolis Star." Library FactFiles. IndyStar.com website.

[102] Feb. 4, 1958. "Sick, Harried Ex-Gangster In Washoe Jail." *Reno Evening Gazette* (Reno, Nev.). 1; Art Long. Feb. 4, 1958. "Ex-Hoodlum Comes Out of Hiding in Nevada." *Nevada State Journal* (Reno, Nev.). 8; and Feb. 10, 1958. "Parole Violator Returns But Story Fails to Check." *Reno Evening Gazette* (Reno, Nev.). 11.

than a decade to August 1970. At that point his mother's obituary listed him as one of the survivors, which he was in more ways than one.[103]

There's a chance he's still alive at the age of 112, here in the year 2010, but it's extremely unlikely. When he died isn't known. While most of the Southern Illinois gangsters who made it at least into middle age can be found through Social Security death records, if Pulliam ever had a number under his real name, it doesn't show up. All that's known for certain is that he didn't die at Menard. Whatever other secrets about the Herrin Gangs, both the Sheltons' and Charlie Birger's, he took with him to the grave.

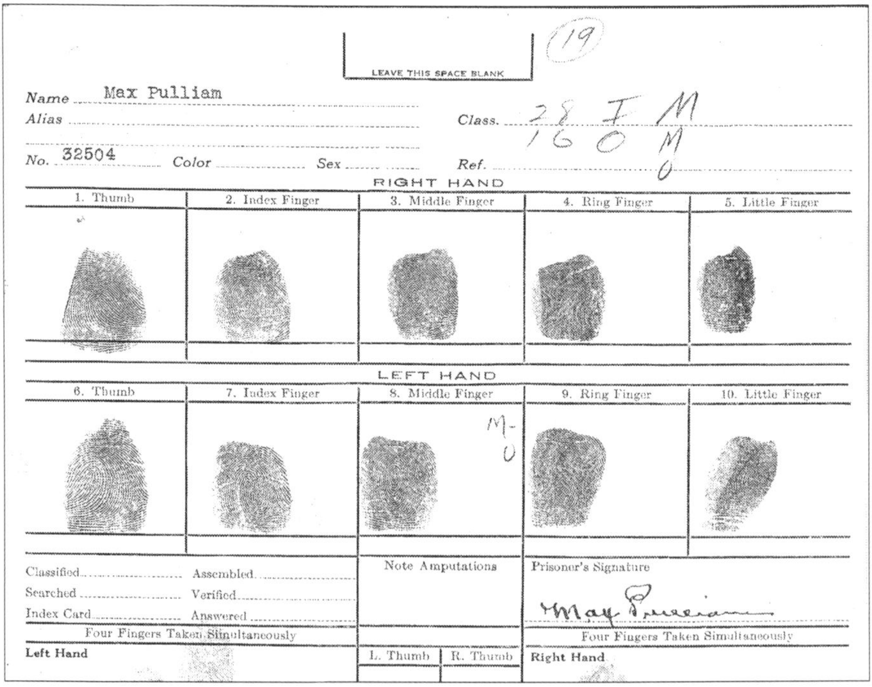
LEAVE THIS SPACE BLANK
(19)
Name Max Pulliam
Alias
Class. 28 I M / 16 O M
No. 32504 Color Sex
Ref. 0
RIGHT HAND
1. Thumb | 2. Index Finger | 3. Middle Finger | 4. Ring Finger | 5. Little Finger
LEFT HAND
6. Thumb | 7. Index Finger | 8. Middle Finger | 9. Ring Finger | 10. Little Finger
M-0
Classified | Assembled | Note Amputations | Prisoner's Signature
Searched | Verified
Index Card | Answered
Max Pulliam
Four Fingers Taken Simultaneously | Four Fingers Taken Simultaneously
Left Hand | L. Thumb | R. Thumb | Right Hand

Pulliam's fingerprints from his Leavenworth file.

[103] Aug. 9, 1970. "Mrs. Nora B. Pulliam Dies Here Friday." newspaper clipping. 1970 Obituary Scrapbook. Frankfort Area Genealogical Society. West Frankfort, Illinois.

Index

Excerpt from

Inside the Shelton Gang: One Daughters Discovery

by Ruthie Shelton and Jon Musgrave

Published in 2013 by IllinoisHistory.com

Chapter 1.

The Big Reveal

"I've been kidnapped!"

Pop's voice was low and raspy, "They've got me tied up. I'm on a dock. You've got to come and get me."

This was the voice on the other end of the phone every night after I got home from a long, exhausting day, sitting at my dad's bedside in the hospital. As soon as I got in my house the phone would ring and the nurse would say, "You have to try and calm your dad down." The nurse put the phone to his ear and the same conversation would be repeated night after night.

I would watch the sun rise in my rear view mirror as I drove away from my home on Black Hammock Island in Jacksonville on Florida's Atlantic coast every morning. Scenes of orange and yellow filled the sky with a peaceful, calming, feeling. But what I was headed for had no peacefulness or calmness about it. My destination was like driving into hurricane force winds. For all of my life this had been my home. I was born and raised among these palm trees and sand dunes. My roots sank deep here, or so I thought. Trees in shallow soil don't fare well in storms. The storm still raged in that bed and what it would reveal would shake me to my core.

Driving back to the hospital each day I hoped I would find my dad awake and alert. It wrenched my heart to see him in that hospital bed. His tanned skin turned pale and his baby blues lacked their luster and vibrancy. He could see, but just not me. He wasn't blind, but he didn't see what was actually there. In his mind he had gone back to a different place and time. He saw people as clearly as if they were standing in front of him, but they weren't. He saw places he hadn't been to in over 50 years, just as real as if he were standing there today.

Pop, as we call my dad, had barely survived surgery and now he didn't know where he was. He kept trying to get out of the bed, to "escape" as he would say. The doctors had to keep him strapped down for his own safety. "You have to get me out of here," he said repeatedly. I kept trying to tell him that he had to stay in the hospital bed but he didn't understand, "No. They're trying to kill us. We have to go, now!"

Every time I left the room he would call out for me, "Ruthie, get me out of here! Somebody get my daughter. Get Ruthie!"

Thus began a week of incoherent ramblings and delusions. There were to be revelations that would forever change my life and change who I am. These unexpected disclosures would answer questions about my own life that I had long since given up on ever knowing the truth about. A course of events was about to unfold that would bring Pop's life full circle. The drugs that had relaxed his body for surgery had broken through decades-old barriers and cautions. The anesthesia had left him temporarily living in the past, his past, a past I knew nothing about. He was now about to inadvertently share with me the life he had left behind a half century before. Most importantly, the end result would reunite him with his first daughter, my sister, Elaine, after a lifetime apart!

I was born into a war that I never knew existed. I was protected, sheltered, hidden, even trained. My mother's instructions to me were, "always check for wires before opening the front door of the house." No explanation was given. I had learned to ask no questions. I did as I was told. I now know that she lived in fear my whole life, fear for her safety, terror for mine. This fear escalated, especially after she and my dad were divorced. When I was 15 my mother told me she had papers drawn up to "give me away." It didn't seem to me that it mattered where I went as long as it was "away." And I didn't know why. But it never happened. My dad stepped in and made sure I was okay.

This was a war that was supposed to have ended in 1951. It played out in the Midwest. The town was named Fairfield, not a name you would expect for the story that was about to be told to me. Fairfield lies in Wayne County, Illinois. By that time, only one side would show themselves openly, the other would be identified by police, sheriffs and the FBI, as "person or persons unknown." This war continued beyond the deaths of all the major players and affected, touched, shaped, even controlled the lives of the next generation, and, unfortunately, the one to follow – mine.

It was the winter of 2003, Pop had been feeling excessively tired. He had no energy at all, he just wanted to sleep all the time. I just thought it was because he was getting older. He liked to tell people he was "going on 80 years old." This was the opposite of how he had lived his life up until the last year or so. He was always busy, running around with his grandchildren, taking care of his animals, working in the yard, helping his neighbors with whatever project they had going, he just never sat still. He was always the first to be ready when there was a trip to take. Over the years he traveled across the country and back with me and my family, many times.

The news from the doctor was crushing to me, Pop needed to have his heart valve replaced. Open heart surgery was required! I didn't think it was a good idea to have such an extensive surgery at 79 years old. But Pop faced this surgery as he lived his life. He hit the problem head on. He never hesitated, "Let's do it!" he told the doctor.

The arrangements were made and all too quickly the day of the surgery came. Pop was very optimistic. He was sure this operation would return him to the life he had always lived. I didn't want him to have the surgery. I was so afraid it would turn out badly. After all, I'd rather have the tired Pop with us than lose him, even if he couldn't do the things he had always loved. But I never told him how I felt. It was his decision to make and I didn't want to influence him.

As we sat in the surgical waiting room in the hospital the hours drug by. Pop's girlfriend and companion of 20 years, Nell, sat nervously by me. "The woman who tamed Pop" is what we call her. Pop was always popular with the ladies. After he and my mother divorced he had a different girlfriend every time I turned around, usually he had two girlfriends at a time. The one he was dating openly and one on the side, "just in case," as Pop would say. Usually, the "one on the side" had money, a lot of money. His woman chasing days ended after he met Nell. Pop's "Nell" was the only lady in his life from then on, he loved her.

My husband, James, was there with me. We have been married since January 1977, and have four children together, Missi, J.C., (James Carl), Jenny and Krystin. Waiting for news in a hospital is never easy and they tried to keep the mood light. Someone pulled out a deck of cards. Never in my life has a family member been in the hospital that card playing wasn't involved. Cards were dealt, flipped and thrown down. Food and drinks came and went. As the morning turned into afternoon no distraction was enough to keep me from feeling that something was terribly wrong.

Every time the doors of the waiting room opened I jumped to my feet hoping that it was Pop's surgeon. But time and again it wasn't. Other families were awaiting news just like we were, and their doctors' came in, gave them their updates and left. And we sat waiting. Watching the clock on the wall, it seemed the hands never moved. I had the ominous feeling that my life was about to take a dramatic change, little did I know how dramatic it would be!

Recently, as I was putting the finishing touches on my book, I realized that some of my memories of that day are a little blurred. So I returned to Memorial Hospital in Jacksonville to try and relive what I could from that day. It's amazing what the sights, sounds and smells of an experience can bring back to the memory.

I parked at the nearby bank, as I did every day Pop was a patient there. It was easier than the hospital parking garage, that seemed too confining. I walked across the parking lot as I did all those days ago. I walked through the entrance to the hospital, spoke to the dear little ladies at the information desk, and walked, very slowly, toward the coronary waiting room. I didn't know exactly what to expect. But through this whole experience, I haven't known what to expect and everything that has happened, to me, to Pop, has so exceeded anything I could ever have imagined!

As I walked into the waiting room, I was greeted by the hospital patient liaison person. He explained to me that he is the person who intercedes between the doctor and the patient's family. This would have been the liaison who let us know when Pop was put on the bypass machine which worked for his heart and lungs during the surgery. He said to me, "I love my job. It's great!"

I told him why I was there. My dad had open heart surgery a few years ago and revealed his hidden past to me as he regained consciousness, after being unconscious for five days. I told him I was writing a book about my dad's family and my experience of discovering all about his past. He told me to take all the time I needed.

The waiting room was large and open. It was quiet, except for the TV showing local news and weather. How much louder it must have been the day my family was there waiting for news of Pop. I could hear the coffee machine running in the background, I could smell the aroma. It reminded me of just how much coffee I drank the day of Pop's surgery and the days of waiting to follow.

One little, older lady sat there alone. This reminded me of Nell. This lady wore tan slacks and a cream colored blouse with a matching sweater. Her hair was cut similar to Nell's. I wondered who she was waiting to hear about. If it was the love of her life like Nell was waiting to hear about hers. I felt so bad for this lady, waiting alone. I could hear people talking and laughter in the distance. There was no laughter the day I waited to hear about Pop, if there was, I didn't hear it.

This day I looked around at the nice furnishings, something I definitely wouldn't have noticed before. The pictures hanging on the walls are of palm trees and coconuts in a beach scene. Some are of the Florida wetlands with egrets taking flight in front of the palm trees. Quite appropriate for living so close to the beach.

As I left the waiting room, I stopped to thank the liaison.

"I've already googled your name and read some about your family," he told me.

I felt a chill go down my spine. Even at this late stage of the writing process, the words Pop had long engraved in my brain, were still echoing in my ears, "Don't let 'em know who you are!"

Other Books by IllinoisHistory.com

The Bloody Vendettas of Illinois Series

The Bloody Vendetta of Southern Illinois by Milo Erwin and Jon Musgrave. The family feuds and Klan activities of the 1870s first gave the name "Bloody" to Williamson County. 240 pages, paperback, $14.95.

Secrets of the Herrin Gangs by Ralph Johnson and Jon Musgrave. An inside account of Bloody Williamson from a Shelton gangster with additional material by Musgrave. 104 pages, paperback. $9.95.

Inside the Shelton Gang by Ruthie Shelton, a daughter's discovery of her family's infamous history. She never knew her family's criminal past until one day in the hospital when her elderly father started telling secrets. 256 pages, paperback, $18.95.

Egyptian Tales of the Heartland by Jon Musgrave, an anthology of the unexpected in the region's history of Southern Illinois, southern Indiana, western Kentucky and southeast Missouri. **Due out in late 2014.**

Southern Illinois History

The Boy of Battle Ford by W. S. Blackman with a new introduction, footnotes and index by Jon Musgrave. This Southern Illinois classic tells Blackman's story of growing up on the frontier in the 1840s and 50s before going off to battle in the Civil War with the 120th Illinois Infantry. First published in 1906. 240 pages, paperback. $18.

History, Mystery and Hauntings of Southern Illinois by Bruce L. Cline. Pulled from the files of the Little Egypt Ghost Society this 2nd edition omnibus version of his first three volumes provides an updated and expanded version of the stories, ghost hunts and folklore that of numerous sites around the region. 320 pages, paperback, $23.95.

Slaves, Salt, Sex & Mr. Crenshaw by Jon Musgrave. The real story of the Old Slave House and America's Reverse Underground Railroad. 608 pages, paperback, $29.95. **Due out in late 2014.**

More books and ordering information on the next page.

Southern Illinois History

The Handbook of Old Gallatin County and Southeastern Illinois, edited by Jon Musgrave. 19th and early 20th Century history. 456 pages, $24, paperback.

Lincoln: Fresh from Abraham's Bosom, edited by Jon Musgrave. Collection of humorous stories and tales told by Abraham Lincoln during the Civil War from his years in the White House. Also includes the First and Second Inaugural Addresses as well as the Gettysburg Address. 80 pgs, paperback, $6.95.

Posters

Warring 20s in Southern Illinois, designed by Jon Musgrave using Alvis Mitchell's famous photograph of Charlie Birger and his gang on the porch of Shady Rest. Colorized with identification of all 16 gang members and a timeline of the major events of the Warring 20s. 18" x 24", $18.

Ordering Information

Order online at **www.IllinoisHistory.com/books**, or mail your order to IllinoisHistory.com, PO Box 1142, Marion IL 62959.

For shipping and handling costs, please add $3 for orders under $10; $4 for orders between $10 and under $25; $4.50 for orders between $25 and under $50; $5 for orders $50 to under $100; and $6 for orders over $100. S/H for posters are $4 in addition to any book orders as posters are shipped in a tube separately.

Illinois residents please add 8.5% sales tax.

For mail orders please include a phone number and/or e-mail address for better communication.